GW00669983

WLA
104S

Graham Robson

CONTENTS

ISBN 0 85429 341 8

A FOULIS Motoring Book

First published 1983

Published by:
Haynes Publishing Group
Sparkford, Yeovil,
Somerset BA22 7JJ

Distributed in USA by:
Haynes Publications Inc.
861 Lawrence Drive, Newbury
Park, California 91320 USA

Cover design: Rowland Smith
Page Layout: Teresa Woodside
Colour photographs: Roger Perry
Road tests: Courtesy of *Motor*
Printed in England by: J.H.Haynes
& Co. Ltd

Titles in the *Super Profile* series

BSA Bantam (F333)
MV Agusta America (F334)
Norton Commando (F335)
Honda CB750 sohc (F351)
Sunbeam S7 & S8 (F363)
BMW R69 & R69S (F387)

Austin-Healey 'Frogeye' Sprite (F343)
Ferrari 250GTO (F308)
Fiat X1/9 (F341)
Ford GT40 (F332)
Jaguar E-Type (F370)
Jaguar D-Type & XKSS (F371)
Jaguar Mk 2 Saloons (F307)
Lancia Stratos (F340)
Lotus Elan (F330)
MGB (F305)
MG Midget & Austin-Healey Sprite (except 'Frogeye') (F344)
Morris Minor & 1000 (ohv) (F331)
Porsche 911 Carrera (F311)
Triumph Stag (F342)

B29 Superfortress (F339)
Boeing 707 (F356)
Harrier (F357)
Phantom II (F376)
Sea King (F377)
Super Etendard (F378)

Further titles in this series will be published at regular intervals. For information on new titles please contact your bookseller or write to the publisher.

FOREWORD

I was enthralled by the Fiat X1/9 from the moment I first set eyes on it, and I have never lost my enthusiasm for it. In terms of numbers built, it is the most successful mid-engined car the world has ever seen, and most X1/9 drivers rave about their cars. It has been called a 'baby Ferrari' too often for me to invent the phrase as my own, but I can quite see why the combination of Bertone styling, Fiat-developed roadholding, and sheer Italian *brio,* makes the description inevitable. The miracle is that it has sold so well, and for so many years, in spite of the very doubtful quality and long-life reputation which Fiat had at the beginning of the period.

This *Super Profile* charts the progress of the X1/9, from being a private Bertone project, to being 'sold' to Fiat; to launch, success, maturity and now, it seems, to decline. It was not at all the sort of car that Fiat had been used to building in the 1960s, and there is evidence to suggest that, even when it was a sales success in North America and elsewhere, they did not really understand it.

The fact is that Bertone did a wonderful job of 'packaging' such a small car, to be so beautiful and at the same time so practical. Before the X1/9 arrived, mid-engined cars in general had had a hard time in the market place. Either they were massive, expensive, incredibly fast Supercars like the Lamborghini Miura or the Maserati Bora, or awkwardly styled like the VW-Porsche 914s; everyone agreed that mid-engined cars were usually less spacious, less versatile, and more costly to build than the 'classic' sports car of MG, Triumph or Alfa Romeo type. The X1/9 (and, to a lesser extent, its 'big sister' the Lancia Monte Carlo) changed that thinking. To this British enthusiast and historian, it is still a mystery that MG were never allowed to build such a car (the AD021) of their own; if they had, the MG marque might still be in existence in the 1980s.

Fiat effectively hived-off the X1/9 at the beginning of the 1980s, when they arranged that Bertone should not only build the body/chassis structures, but complete assembly of the whole car as well. Since the same sort of deal was made with Pininfarina over the 124 Spider, I take this as a signal that Fiat are now getting out of the sports car business for good. Certainly, at this moment, there is no sign of a successor to the X1/9 – which is very sad news, but which means that owners should enjoy, and cherish, their X1/9s for as long as they can.

Two such owners, who cheerfully made their cars available for photography, are Brian Thompson (who owns a 1300) and Joel Sciamma (whose love is a 1500 5-speed), and I'd like to thank them publicly for making this book possible; they also helped me with a digest of owners' views about the cars.

Bertone of Turin very kindly let me look around their factory at one stage, and I am also grateful to Graham Gauld, Fiat Auto (UK) Ltd, and the staff at the Centro Storico in Turin for their help over archive material, and statistics.

Lastly, of course, I am indebted to those magazines who gave permission for road tests and other long-term reports to be reproduced, so that we could complete the scope of information in this book. Without them, the British motoring enthusiast would have great difficulty in ever finding unbiased opinion about new cars.

A.A.G.R.

HISTORY

Ever since Fiat introduced the cheeky little 995cc Balilla Sport in 1932, they have been famous for building nicely-detailed and nimble sports cars with rather small engines. After the Balilla there was the 508CMM, then the post-war 1100s which evolved from it, the 1100 Trasformabile, and then the Pininfarina 1200s and Osca-engined machines which succeeded that car. All the time, however, the cars were gradually, but inexorably, getting larger. In the 1960s, it was time to start again.

A whole new family of Fiats then grew from Dr. Dante Giacosa's brilliantly-original rear-engined 600 saloon of 1955. The larger 850 evolved from it in 1964, and it was on the basis of that all-independently sprung floorpan that Fiat produced a chunky little coupe of their own, and on which Bertone, with factory backing, built the marvellously-sleek little 850 Spider. From 1965 to 1973, Bertone churned out 132,546 of these wedge-nosed open two-seaters, most of which were sold in North America.

In the meantime, however, Fiat were turning to front-wheel-drive for their next generation of small saloon cars. The original f.w.d. Fiat production car was actually badged as an Autobianchi (the Primula), but the first *official* front-drive Fiat was the 128 of 1969.

Like most 'standard Euroboxes' of the period, the 128 had a four-cylinder water-cooled engine, transversely-mounted, and driving the front wheels. Where it broke new ground, however, is that the engine had single overhead camshaft valve gear, while the new four-speed gearbox was mounted at the end of the (transverse) engine, rather than behind or underneath it. Naturally this car also had all-independent suspension, and it soon came to be sold in a variety of body styles, and engine ratings.

In the long-term scheme of things, Fiat had not only decided to build a higher-powered 1.3-litre 'Rally' saloon, but to develop a two-door 128 Coupe with 1.1-litre and 1.3-litre engine options, which would directly replace the well-liked 850 Sport Coupe. Although they were willing to let the obsolescent rear-engined 850 Spider carry on for a time, they also wanted to see this replaced by a new 128-based car.

Even though it took time, this was the point at which the X1/9 project began to take shape – but not at first. Bertone, who had the 850 Spider business, were anxious to retain their links with Fiat over the new model family, so in 1968/1969, even before the basic 128 Saloon was revealed, they began trying to develop a new 128 Spider – with a front-engine and front-wheel-drive.

The Bertone-styled 128 Spider, however, was not a success, for the famous Italian styling house found the same problem which had defeated BMC/BL designers when they had tried to produce an acceptable Mini sports car – the front engine/transmission power pack just would not allow a smart enough body style to be wrapped around it. Even though they refined their 128 Spider as much as possible, it did not meet their own requirements. Accordingly, and as a private venture, they had heretical thoughts – and looked at a mid-engined concept instead!

Nuccio Bertone himself authorised such a layout, for his designers had already produced fine mid-engined designs for Lamborghini (the Miura and the Marzal), and thought they could do just as good a job on a smaller scale. It was their genius, echoed by the MG designers a couple of years later, which caused an entire transverse engine, transmission and basic suspension from the front-wheel-drive car to be moved 'in space', and installed neatly behind the seats of a new Spider. At a stroke, here was a new car which could not only be made to look sensational, but one which would be fashionably like the current breed of racing sports cars, of which the Ferrari 512 and Porsche 917 were merely the latest and most exciting examples.

Bertone staff have told me that they showed both the front-engine/front-wheel-drive 128 Spider project, and their own mid-engined style to Fiat management, and that for a time the 'conventional' (by Fiat's new standards) front-drive car was favoured. However, to get a taste of the public's opinion, Bertone then produced a special 'show car' for Turin in November 1969. This car started out as the Fiat mid-engined proposal, with a hurriedly-constructed open two-seater body shell, but eventually appeared with a pushrod ohv 903cc Fiat/Autobianchi engine in the transverse A112 installation.

The Runabout was well received (although *Autocar* completely missed the fact that the engine was behind the seats!) at the show, and because it was merely thought to be a 'Dream Car', no-one ever expected it to run, or ever to be seen again. Certainly it never was seen again in that form, for Bertone soon re-installed the Fiat 128 engine/transmission pack, and eventually made the car into a running prototype. Eventually, Bertone (and, it must be admitted, Fiat's President, Giovanni Agnelli!) got their way, and the new mid-engined concept was officially taken up by Fiat as their '850 Spider replacement'. It would take a long time, however, before the new car, coded X1/9, would be ready for sale – not only the exigencies of testing, development, and tooling, but the problems of meeting North American safety regulations, would see to that. The breakdown of responsibilities, however, was quite clear. Bertone, who were not only world-famous stylists, but were now capable of producing specialised bodies in considerable quantities, were contracted to press, assemble, paint and trim the entire unit-construction body/chassis unit, at their newest factory situated in Grugliasco, a suburb of Turin, only about five kilometres west of the main Fiat assembly plant at Mirafiori. Fiat, for their part, would complete assembly of the cars, road test them, and distribute them all over the world. The Bertone badge would be displayed on each and every car built.

It is worth noting that when this new mid-engined sports car was coming on stream at Bertone, it would take shape alongside cars as distinguished as the Alfa Romeo Montreal, the Fiat Dino Coupe, and the Lamborghini Urraco.

While all this preparatory work was going on, however, Fiat and Bertone were shocked to see another car appear at the Turin Show of November 1971 – one which had nothing to do with them, but one which looked amazingly similar to the new Fiat, still secret and unannounced! The car in question was on the DeTomaso stand, was called the DeTomaso 1600, and had been shaped by Tom Tjaarda at Ghia.

The fact that the two cars looked very similar was no coincidence, nor was the similarity uncanny. According to DeTomaso historian Wallace Wyss, Alejandro DeTomaso had merely seen sneak sketches of the new Bertone car, when these had been published in Italian motoring magazines, then directed Ghia (a styling house which he owned) to build an 'identikit' style on the rolling chassis which he had shown in Turin a year earlier.

The DeTomaso project was powered by a transversely-mounted 16-valve twin-cam Ford BDA engine (as fitted to the RS1600 rally car), which was placed behind the passengers, so it was easy enough for Tjaarda, a very accomplished stylist, to produce a similar shape. It was, in every way, as smart and potentially practical – but then, Bertone's styling engineers had already done the ground work on which the talented Tjaarda could develop the theme. In the long term, however, Fiat and Bertone had no cause to worry, as DeTomaso never took their project any further, and even the original prototype has now disappeared.

Once the Bertone style, and mechanical layout, had been adopted officially by Fiat, it was given a code. As a project, as in production form, this car was always known as the X1/9. For years there was great speculation as to the meaning, or the significance, of such a code – for all recent new Fiats had carried names like 124, 125 and, of course, 128. It was not until Dr. Giacosa's autobiography was published that it was revealed that an alternative series of Fiat project codes had existed for some time. X1/1, the first, had actually referred to the 128 saloon, while X1/3 was the big 130 saloon.

The design of the production car, of course, centred on the location, and installation, of the transverse engine and transmission. In the Fiat 128 Coupe, which used the same 75bhp engine tune, 1,290cc engine size, and four-speed transmission, the power pack was at the front of the car driving the front wheels, whereas in the X1/9 it was behind the two seats, in the 'mid' position, and driving the rear wheels. It is not generally realised, however, that to suit the X1/9 installation the whole block/transmission was rotated to a slightly more upright position (with cylinder axes just 11 degrees forward of vertical) – which made access to the sparking plugs that important bit easier – that the distributor layout and drive was changed from the 128, and that the top gear ratio was slightly raised (from 1.037:1 to 0.959:1 inside the box) without changing the final drive ratio. The major change required, of course, was to the gear selection linkage. In the front-drive 128 installation, this had been fed out of the rear of the transmission casing, towards a lever between the front seats. For the X1/9, of course, the linkage had to be brought *forward,* to a lever between the seats, which were ahead of the installation. Apart from manifold and mounting differences however, this was the sum total of the work needed, and as Bertone provided a large lift-up engine cover immediately behind the cabin, access for service and maintenance was perfectly satisfactory.

The kernel of the design of course, was the styling, and the structure of the body shell. Except that this had to incorporate a transverse mid-mounted engine, the shell was a conventional pressed-steel monocoque, wedge-styled, with flip-up headlamps at the front corners, high front bumpers and a prominent spoiler, and what looked like a conventional coupe style.

Close inspection however, showed not only that Bertone had found space for two luggage lockers – one in the nose, and one behind the engine/transmission installation – but they had also arranged for the entire top roof panel to be detached, and for stowage, if needed, to fit snugly in the front 'boot', under the opening panel. There was, indeed, much to open, flap up, or take away on an X1/9. If you tried, you could have headlamps erect, the front boot lid open, the roof panel off (or coming off), the engine lid open, the rear boot lid open, *and* both doors wide open. The miracle therefore, was that the basic structure was so rigid, and the 'chassis platform' so stable.

Most of the strength of the body shell was in the floor, where box section sills under the doors, and a central 'service tunnel' (there was no propeller shaft, of course) provided beam strength. Torsional rigidity was helped along by a front bulkhead which held the cooling radiator, the toeboard/scuttle ahead of the passengers, the bulkhead behind the seats which supported the coupe pillars and provided a housing for the spare wheel, and by two more bulkheads, one behind the engine, and one in the extreme tail. It was no wonder, not only that this compact little car could meet all known and projected USA crash test and roll-over legislation, but that it was significantly heavier than the 128 Coupe which was really its more conventional model relative.

The suspension layout, which was all independent, was interesting. At the front, the MacPherson strut layout was like that of the 128 saloon, except that there was no provision for the front-drive drive shafts. At the rear, too, was MacPherson strut independent suspension, utilising the original 128 drive shafts, and hubs, but with a massive, fabricated, semi-trailing lower wishbone, and an extra locating link which looked as if it tied up to the redundant (front-drive) steering arm, but did not, in fact.

Rack and pinion steering of 128 type was fitted, but there was no need for anti-roll bars at front or rear. Completing the basic chassis were front *and* rear disc brakes, both like the front brakes of the 128 saloon, and pressed-steel four-stud fixing wheels with 4.5in wide rims, and 145-13in radial ply tyres.

The neatness and space-saving ideas in this design were perfectly demonstrated behind the two seats. On the left side, behind the usual position of the driving seat, was the 10.8 gallon fuel tank (with its filler tucked away in a corner behind one of the coupe body pillars), and on the right side, matching it, and with a fold down cover into the passenger compartment, was the location of the spare wheel. This meant that there was significantly more space for luggage in the front 'boot' than is found on some other mid-engined cars. On right-hand-drive cars, of course, this spare wheel found itself behind the driver's seat, but this proved to be no disadvantage, as punctures are so rare these days.

There were initial worries, incidentally, that this wheel location would be unsuitable for slightly-built girls to remove the spare. Accordingly, as Philip Turner of *Motor* once wrote: 'Bertone rounded up some of their more shapely girl secretaries and set them to extracting the spare wheel. This they did with far less trouble than when having to bend over to remove the wheel from its normal position in or under the boot'.

I should make it quite clear that while the style of the car was by Bertone, on Fiat's behalf, the engineering, and detail touches, were all by Fiat's team, led for Dr. Giacosa by Guiseppe Puleo, who was then the director of advanced design. Much of the development work went into two areas – reducing the weight of the car to a practical (and safe) minimum, and to getting enough air into the cooling radiator without destroying the car's looks, or its aerodynamic efficiency. The large front spoiler, therefore, had as much to do with forcing air up into the cooling ducts, as it did in keeping air from flowing under the body shell. About the car's weight, however, there was little that could be done. In the end, the 12ft 7in long two-seater 'Targa' coupe weighed 65kg (144lb) more than the 128 Coupe, which had four seats and was almost exactly the same length – much of this penalty can be blamed on the extra structure needed to satisfy USA legislation, the rest on the need to bolster up a body shell with so many opening panels – six if you count the doors and the removable roof.

The layout, and detail, of the interior, was everything that one might expect of a Bertone style. The seats, of course, could not be made to recline because they were right up against the spare wheel/petrol tank bulkhead when at the back of their adjustment, but they were well-shaped (if plastic covered) with built-in headrests. There was a comprehensive heating and ventilation installation and (for the USA only) a power-sapping full air-conditioning option.

The driving position, as expected, was excellent, the driver finding the gearlever in an ideal position, the hand-brake lever behind it, on top of the services tunnel, and a four-spoke steering wheel ahead of him. A centre console housing ventilation controls, vents and switches, was standard, while the instrument pack included crescent-style speedometer and rev-counter dials all behind a single pane of glass. There was a glove box ahead of the passenger's knees, but it was tiny and of limited use.

It took a long time for the new X1/9 to be brought from project, to prototype, to series production – the Bertone 'Runabout', after all, had appeared in public in November 1969 – but Fiat were still not prepared to show the new car at their own Turin Show of November 1972. In different times, or in another year, perhaps they *would* have shown the car, for production was just beginning. On this occasion, however, they wanted the public to concentrate on the new 126 baby saloon, and on the new 132 medium-sized saloon, both of which cars were commercially much more important in the huge Italian domestic market.

Accordingly, the new small Fiat sports car, which was positively brimming over with interesting new features, was launched immediately after the Turin Show, actually on 23 November 1972, just as the first few cars were being completed. At the time it was priced at a mere 1,800,000 lire (about £1,250) in Italy, which compared with 1,450,000 (about £1,000) for the 128 Coupe 1300, and made it look a very attractive proposition for the Americans, when they could get their hands on it.

For a time the old 850 Spider, now under notice of execution, remained in production, for the X1/9 was still not ready and approved for sale in North America. The new car would not go on sale until the 1974 model year, and therefore the Spider continued to be built until mid-1973.

The motoring press, and the public, simply loved the X1/9. Apart from the moaners who thought it should be cheaper and/or faster, no one had a bad word to say about it. Fiat's press introduction, in Sicily on the Targa Florio course, resulted in wide-spread praise, and several unintentional demonstrations of the car's strength in accidents! The only problem, of course, was that sales were confined to Italy in the first year, and (for we British) that sales here did not begin until 1977.

For example, *Road Test* of the USA called it a 'Mid-Engine Classic' even before it went on sale in that country, while (three years later, admittedly) *Road & Track* commented that : 'Anyone who would buy an MG Midget when the X1/9 was available for only $1,000 more would have to be a complete masochist.' When *Autocar's* Peter Windsor was priviliged to use an X1/9 for 24,000 miles in 1977 and 1978, he summed up his first (12,000 mile) report in just three words : 'A baby Ferrari'.

Even though the X1/9 had one big advantage – that it was launched at a time when all its competitors (the Midget, the Spitfire, the smaller-engined Alfas, and the Lancia Fulvia, for instance) were old-fashioned, ageing and somehow beginning to look prehistoric – it was still one hell of a car. Its original price in the USA at the beginning of 1974 was $3,970 (£1,655 in British currency – though, don't forget, there was no Special Car Tax or VAT in North America) which made it an all-round bargain – with a 95mph top speed even in de-toxed form it would surely become a Best Seller, just so long as the quality control was right.

In looks, in layout, and in road behaviour, it was so far ahead of the competition that Fiat had no need to set about designing 'Mk II' versions right away, which explains why the original X1/9 1300 went on, virtually unchanged, until the autumn of 1978, by which time nearly 100,000 X1/9s had been built. Nevertheless, it was infuriating to the British, the Australians, and other outposts of the right-hand-driving 'Empire' that they could not have the X1/9s at first. In Britain, Fiat-specialists Radbourne Racing produced a right-hand-drive conversion which, complete with cast-alloy wheels and larger tyres, sold for nearly £2,800. (This, incidentally, compared badly with Midget or Spitfire prices, and when *Motor* tested one they felt obliged to compare it with the £2,508 MG MGB GT V8, which had a 3.5-litre engine!).

In the meantime, however, Fiat set about developing a 'Big Brother' version of the X1/9, this time with a Pininfarina style, and this time with a transversely-mounted Lancia Beta (which really meant Fiat, anyway) engine and transmission. Until a late stage this was going to be badged as a Fiat, and was provisionally dubbed X1/20 by the know-alls, but it eventually became the Lancia Monte Carlo, and has not had nearly as much success. Fiat's competitions specialists, Abarth, which had become a wholly-owned subsidiary, also dabbled with the X1/9, and managed to squeeze the Beta/Monte Carlo power pack into the normal engine bay. Along with fatter wheels, flared wheel arches, and a saucy engine intake scoop sprouting from the engine bay lid, the result was a prototype Group 4 rally car which might, just might, have been able to beat the in-house competition from the Lancia Stratos, but which was abandoned in favour of the 131 Abarth saloon car project. Half a dozen prototypes had already been made, and Abarth were completing the tooling for a 400-off production run to take place in 1975, when the project was cancelled.

To round off the minimal 'competitions X1/9' story, I should add that ex-Lamborghini, ex-Stratos, ex-DeTomaso designer Giampaolo Dallara started developing a Group 5 racing X1/9 in 1973 for 'silhouette' racing, where it was to come complete with a 16-valve cylinder head. This became a competitive machine in its class, where the regulations allowed, but it was never a 'works' project, and now seems to be over its peak.

The production life of the X1/9, though long and honourable, can quite easily be told, for in its first ten years the car was never offered with any alternative body styles, or with major restyling done to it, nor did it benefit from major mechanical transplants. Until the 1979 model year (which really meant that new cars started to be built in the autumn of 1978), all X1/9s had the same 1,290cc engine, which was marginally de-toxed for mid-1970s European emission laws (with power reduced from 75bhp to 73bhp), and which had to be strangled to 66bhp for sale in the USA. Most cars had the relatively narrow pressed steel road wheels and 145-section tyres, though smart cast-alloy wheels and 165/70-section tyres were also available (and standard on UK-market cars).

When the X1/9 was finally

launched in Britain, for 1977, it was in a decidedly upmarket condition, complete with cloth-covered seats, special side striping, cast alloy wheels and fat tyres, a black front spoiler, foglamps and tinted glass, not forgetting the two soft bags provided in the rear luggage boot. The first batch, based on this Bertone *Serie Speciale,* all featured a special numbered plaque on the near side front wing, complete with Union Flag, and Nuccio Bertone's signature, and all for £2,997.

It wasn't long, however, before yet another special-series model, the Lido, was on offer. The X1/9 Lido (the name was taken from that of the night club in Paris) featured black paintwork, chrome bumpers and white seats and trim – not very practical for grubby climates, but very effective as a crowd-puller.

In North America, by the way, the new '5mph crash' regulations, which required the bodyshell to sustain no damage after such a collision, resulted in massive front and rear bumpers being fitted from 1976.

The only major change, however, came in autumn 1978, not only as a significant improvement, but to keep the X1/9 as commonised as possible with the latest new Fiats. In April 1978, the strange-looking Ritmo (Strada in the USA, and in Britain) had been introduced. Its engine and transmission were direct developments of those already used in the 128s and X1/9s, but there were three different engine sizes, the largest of which was the long stroke, 1498cc unit and this not only had a deeper cylinder block, but also incorporated a five-speed gearbox.

For the X1/9, which needed more torque to look after the de-toxing penalties imposed by North America, this derivative looked ideal, so it was speedily adopted. Not only did the X1/9 1500 have 85bhp instead of 73bhp but a great deal more torque (see Specification Tables). In addition, the new five-speed gearbox not only left the bottom three ratios as before, and fourth gear reverting to the slightly lower 128 ratio, but involved a 0.863:1 fifth gear. Overall gearing, therefore, rose from 16.68mph/1,000rpm, to 18.27mph/1,000rpm.

In the USA there had been complaints about the style of the latest '5 mph' bumpers, so for the 1500 a new and much smoother style was provided. For the first time (and for all subsequent X1/9s) this style was also adopted for other-market cars (which were in the minority, in any case), a move which helped standardisation, but slightly increased the length and weight of the cars.

The result was a car which was comfortably quicker, and lustier, than before, but not by as much as USA road tests suggested – this almost certainly being due to a 'super-standard' car being supplied by the importers for important magazines like *Road & Track,* or *Car & Driver,* to wring out. In European terms, however, the X1/9 instantly progressed from being a car which had to be revved very hard, and which struggled to reach 100mph, to one which felt more relaxed to drive, and which had a top speed approaching 110mph instead. It was a measure of our inflationary times that an early-1979 X1/9 1500 cost $7,115 in the USA, and £4,575 in the UK.

The X1/9, however, was now really at the peak of its development, and its popularity, as the engine could not be further enlarged, or the performance further improved (not, that is, without adding more extreme features to the engine itself), without a major transplant. If the car had continued to be such a world-wide success this might, indeed, have happened, but in the meantime a quality-control storm had blown up around Fiat, world-wide, one which produced much adverse publicity and threatened to ruin the Italian concern's reputation. In the UK this was pinpointed by the Lancia Beta scandal, whereas in North America the malaise seemed to be more wide-spread. Owners' surveys carried out by motoring magazines in North America did not help, and the fact that the styling remained unaltered, eight years after the car's launch, was another factor.

Both the 'federalised' Fiat sports cars, the 124 Spider and the X1/9, were affected, such that sales in 1981 slumped alarmingly. Accordingly, Fiat decided to remove final assembly from their own Turin factories, doing a similar deal with Pininfarina and Bertone respectively. Instead of merely building painted and trimmed body/chassis units, the coachbuilders would now take over complete assembly and, eventually, direct marketing and distribution as well. The high point of production – up to 100 shells a day – was past, and for 1982 it was thought that only about 30 to 40 complete cars could be produced in a single day.

At Bertone, complete assembly of X1/9s began in September 1981, of USA-market cars, and by the beginning of 1982 the transition was complete, and the world was told. For 1982, USA market cars were given engines with fuel injection (optional from 1980), and peak power boosted to 75bhp (which brought them back to 1973 levels for *non*USA cars...), while all varieties were given new badging, and became X1/9 IN, where IN meant Injection or, if you preferred it, 'In fashion', or 'In vogue' for other markets. That, at least, is what Bertone told me! Two-tone paintwork was standardised, there was red seating and interior trim, and yet another series of brushed copper name plates on the dashboard, complete with numbers and the famous Bertone signature.

At the time of writing, however, this seems to have been a final, and short-lived fling for the X1/9. On a recent visit to the

Bertone factory at Grugliasco, in September 1982, I not only found that the X1/9 was not being built, but that the assembly lines were empty, and that no partly-built body/chassis units were in evidence either. I most sincerely hope that this was only a major stock-balancing operation (my guide was delightfully vague about the whole business...), and not the end of a very fine car's career. Bertone would not, or could not, provide me with accurate production figures to this point, which seems quite inexplicable, if not evasive.

However, even if the X1/9 story is now complete, the beautiful little Bertone-styled car will still go down in history as a great engineering, if not commercial, success. One cannot have built and sold around 150,000 cars of this type, in what is a rather restricted marketing sector, and be dubbed a failure. By comparison with almost any other mid-engined car (VW-Porsche 914 notwithstanding), the X1/9 was an extremely elegant solution to serious packaging problems. It was a car which not only looked right, but felt right, and behaved impeccably too. Fiat, Bertone, and the enlightened customers, can all feel proud of that.

EVOLUTION

Although the structure and general layout of the X1/9 did not change between 1972 and 1982, there was one major technical upheaval in 1978, and various minor, but significant, changes, made before and after this date:

1972 : The original European-specification X1/9 was announced in November. At first, therefore, all cars had left-hand drive, and pressed-steel road wheels were fitted.

247 bodies built*

1973 : Volume sales of X1/9s began – but no cars were officially sent to Britain, or to the USA.

9,480 bodies built

1974 : Sales of 'Federal' specification cars began in the USA, with de-tuned (66bhp) engines. Increase in production almost exactly matched by USA first-year sales of 10,397.

20,207 bodies built

1975 : No basic, few detail changes. Sales almost entirely concentrated on the USA.

17,318 bodies built

1976 : For USA only, the 'Federal' version was given larger 'safety' bumpers, front and rear.

For the UK, and other 'Empire' markets, a right-hand-drive version was, at last, revealed. For the UK, cast-alloy wheels were standardised.

15,882 bodies built

1977 : Volume sales began in the UK. 'Lido' limited-edition model, with special colour schemes, and trim, also marketed.

18,451 bodies built

1978 : In October, original car replaced by new X1/9 1500 'Five-speed', and all cars now built with nicer-style, still bulky, 'Federal' bumpers. Engine 1,498cc instead of 1,290cc, overall gearing higher, car itself heavier. Externally, a bulkier engine lid gives recognition, internally a new facia, luggage locker, and other details.

19,240 bodies built

1979 : 1500 version on sale in USA, with 67bhp (compared with European car's 85bhp) – Californian version with 66bhp.

20,082 bodies built

1980 : No important changes.

14,993 bodies built

1981 : From mid-1981, complete assembly of X1/9s for the USA 'Federal' market was carried out at the Bertone factory on the outskirts of Turin. X1/9s for other markets were progressively fed into Bertone in later months.

4,619 bodies built

1982 : Complete assembly of all X1/9s taken over by Bertone from Fiat. Mechanically, no changes for rest of World, but for the USA, Bosch fuel-injection (optional from 1980) helped boost power to 75bhp. Cars now known as Bertone X1/9 IN series (not Fiat), where IN stands for Injection in the USA, and for 'In Vogue' or 'In fashion' in Italy.

From autumn 1982, production suspended, and production area at Bertone cleared.

1983 : Sales of X1/9 continued, entirely marketed by Bertone, including the 'VS' (Special Version).

SPECIFICATION

X1/9 1300, as originally produced from 1972

Type designation Type X1/9 sports coupe

Built Turin, Italy, 1972 to 1978

Numbers manufactured Approximately 100,000 (precise figures not available)

Drive configuration Mid-engine, rear drive. Engine transversely mounted behind seats

Engine Fiat Type 128AS.000. Four cylinders, in line, transversely mounted across car. Cast iron cylinder block, with light-alloy cylinder head. Two valves per cylinder, in line, operated by single overhead camshaft, driven by belt from nose of crankshaft. Bore, stroke and capacity 86 x 55.5mm, 1,290cc (3.39 x 2.19 in, 78.7 cu in) 8.9:1 compression ratio
One downdraught dual-choke Weber Type 32 DMTR 22 carburettor
Maximum power 75bhp (DIN) at 6,000rpm. 9.2:1, and 73bhp from 1977 in the UK
Maximum torque 72lb ft at 3,400rpm
(USA version, from 1974) 8.5:1 compression ratio. Maximum power 66bhp at 5,800rpm. Maximum torque 68lb ft at 3,600rpm

Transmission Four-speed Fiat 128 gearbox, in unit with transversely-mounted engine, and final drive. Four forward speeds, with synchromesh on each ratio.
Internal gearbox ratios : 3.583, 2.235, 1.454, 0.959, reverse 3.714:1
Helical spur gear final drive, ratio 13/53 = 4.077:1
Overall fourth gear ratio 3.91:1

Chassis Sheet steel monocoque, combined body/chassis unit, built for Fiat by Bertone of Turin
Wheelbase 7ft 2.75in (220cm)
Track (front) 4ft 4.5in (133.5cm)
Track (rear) 4ft 5.0in (134.5cm)

Suspension	Front : Independent, by coil springs, MacPherson struts, lower wishbones, and telescopic dampers. No anti-roll bar Rear : Independent, by coil springs, MacPherson struts, semi-trailing lower wishbones, and telescopic dampers No anti-roll bar
Steering	Rack and pinion; 3.1 turns lock-to-lock
Brakes	Discs at front and rear, with no vacuum servo assistance. Front discs 8.9in dia; rear discs 8.9in dia. Mechanical operation of centrally-mounted handbrake
Wheels and tyres	Cast-alloy bolt-on road wheels, or pressed-steel bolt-on road wheels, depending on market in which sold, with four-stud fixing, 13in rim diameter, 4.5in rims and 145-13in Pirelli tyres (steel rims) or 5.0in wheel rim width, 165/70SR-13in Pirelli or Michelin radial-ply tyres. (Alloy rims)
Bodywork	All steel body style, with removable 'Targa' type of roof panel (can be stowed in the front luggage compartment), built integrally with load-bearing 'chassis' monocoque, by Bertone of Turin; final assembly by Fiat, also in Turin Dimensions : (European markets) Overall length 12ft 6.75in (383cm); overall width 5ft 1.75in (157cm); overall height 3ft 10in (117cm). Unladen weight 2010lb (913kg). (USA market) Overall length 12ft 9.5in (390cm). Unladen weight 2.156lb (978kg); other dimensions as before
Electrical system	12 volt, 45 amp hr battery. Negative earth system, including Marelli components, and alternator. Ignition by Marelli; Marelli, Bosch or Champion spark plugs
Fuel system	Mid-mounted fuel tank, behind seats, 10.8 (Imperial) gallons (49 litres). Average fuel consumption 31mpg (9.2 litres/100km)
Performance	(European version) Source *Autocar,* 1977: Maximum speed 99mph. Maximum speeds in gears, 3rd gear 77mph; 2nd gear 50mph; 1st gear 31mph. Acceleration : 0-60mph 12.7sec; Standing $\frac{1}{4}$-mile 18.8sec; Acceleration in gears: Top : 20-40mph 11.7sec; 50-70mph 13.5sec. Third : 20-40mph 6.4sec; 50-70mph 8.7sec. Fuel consumption : 28 to 40mpg (Imperial) (USA version) Source *Road & Track,* 1974: Maximum speed 93mph. Maximum speed in gears, 3rd gear 75mph; 2nd gear 49mph; 1st gear 30mph. Acceleration : 0-60mph 15.3sec. Standing $\frac{1}{4}$-mile 20.1sec. Fuel consumption : 30mpg (USA) = 36mpg (Imperial)

X1/9 1500, as produced from autumn 1978

Type designation	X1/9 1500 5-speed
Built	Turin, Italy, 1978 to date
Numbers manufactured	Approximately 50,000 (precise figures not available)

Basic style, design, and layout as for original X1/9 1300, except for following technical differences :

Engine	Bore, stroke and capacity 86.4 x 63.9mm, 1,498cc (3.40 x 2.52in, 91.5cu in). 9.2:1 compression ratio. One downdraught dual-choke

Weber Type 34DATR 7/250 carburettor
Maximum power 85bhp (DIN) at 6,000rpm. Maximum torque 87lb ft at 3,200rpm
(USA version)
8.5:1 compression ratio. Maximum power 67bhp (SAE net) at 5,250rpm. Maximum torque 76lb ft at 3,000rpm

Transmission
Five-speed Fiat Ritmo/Strada gearbox, in unit with transversely-mounted engine and final drive. Five forward speeds, with synchromesh on each ratio. Internal gearbox ratios : 3.583, 2.235, 1.454, 1.042, 0.863, reverse 3.714:1. Helical spur gear final drive ratio, ratio 13/53 = 4.077:1. Overall fifth gear ratio 3.52:1

Wheels and tyres
Pressed-steel (USA), cast-alloy (other markets), both with 5.0in rims, and 165/70SR13in tyres

Bodywork
Overall length (Europe and USA) 13ft 0.3in (397cm). Unladen weight (Europe) 2,010lb (912kg)

Fuel system
Average fuel consumption 26mpg (10.8 litres/100km)

Performance
(European version) Source *Autocar,* 1979 Maximum speed 106mph. Maximum speeds in gears, 4th gear 104mph; 3rd gear 75mph; 2nd gear 49mph; 1st gear 30mph. Acceleration : 0-60mph 11.0sec. Standing $\frac{1}{4}$-mile 17.8sec. Acceleration in gears : Top : 20-40mph 11.7sec; 50-70mph 12.2sec; Fourth : 20-40mph 8.3sec; 50-70mph 9.4sec; Third : 20-40mph 5.4sec; 50-70mph 7.4sec. Fuel consumption : 24 to 34mpg (Imperial)
(USA Federal version) Source *Road & Track,* 1979
Maximum speed 110mph. Maximum speeds in gears : 4th gear 105mph; 3rd gear 78mph; 2nd gear 50mph; 1st gear 32mph
Acceleration : 0-60mph 11.1sec. Standing $\frac{1}{4}$-mile 18.3sec. Fuel consumption : 28mpg (USA) = 33.5mpg (Imperial)
(I suspect that this car was 'super standard')

X1/9 1500 with fuel-injection, as produced for USA in 1982

Basic specification as for 1979-type 'Federal' X1/9 1500 except for following technical differences :

Engine
Bosch L-Jetronic fuel injection.
Maximum power 75bhp (DIN) at 5,500rpm; Maximum torque 79lb ft at 3,000rpm.

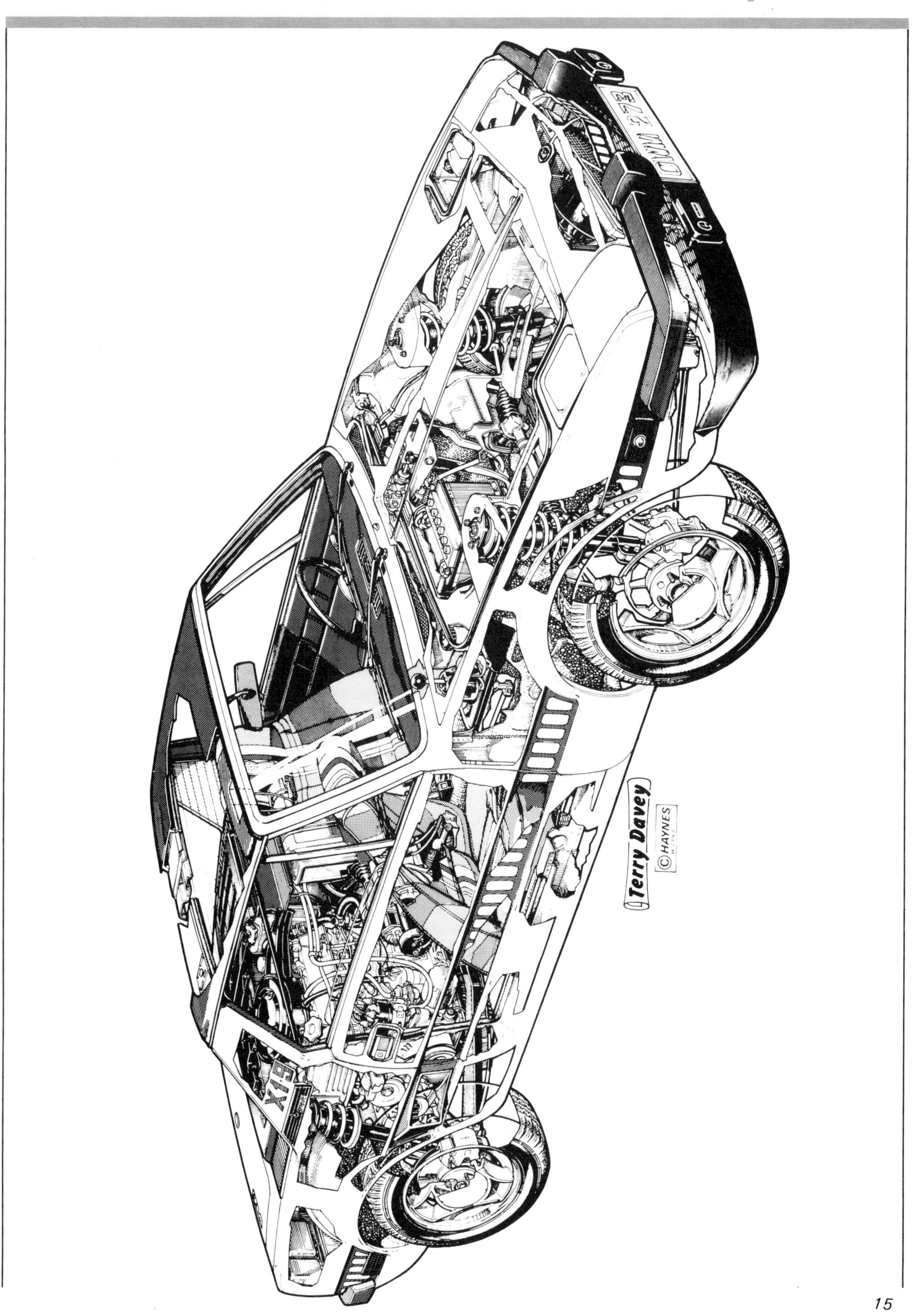
Terry Davey
© HAYNES

ROAD TESTS

MOTOR week ending February 26, 1977

Star Road Test

FIAT X1/9

Fiat's decision to import their pretty little X1/9 two-seater brings a welcome breath of fresh air to Britain's sports car scene. A clever package with excellent handling and good economy it represents the trend in modern sports car design. Refined and with more power it would be even better

AT ITS announcement in 1972, Fiat's Bertone styled X1/9 had the distinction of being the first mid-engined sports car destined for volume production. The road-going designs of Ferrari, Lotus, Maserati and Porsche had all preceded Fiat's pretty little two seater but none was ever intended to match the 100 per day output of the X1/9. Over four years later a challenger has yet to emerge and no fewer than 44,000 X1/9s have already been shipped to the United States alone.

Sadly, there has been no official right-hand drive version during this period, though a laudable attempt to plug the gap was made by Fiat dealer, Radbourne Racing, who imported the cars in LHD form and carried out their own conversion. Inevitably the exercise was expensive and not many were sold. Now at long last a RHD version of the plush X1/9 "Special" is being imported by Fiat at £2998 which is very little higher than the Radbourne car of two years ago.

With all their resources Fiat could easily have produced a cheap yet desirable sports car by rebodying the front-engined 128 saloon, but they chose to do the job properly. The Bertone-styled body is not only strikingly aerodynamic but the designer employs the very principles that have taken racing cars to such heights of traction and cornering power. By placing the uprated 128 engine transversely behind the passenger compartment, though ahead of the rear wheels, he has obtained the degree of rearward weight bias necessary for good traction and confined the major masses well within the axles, thus giving the low polar moment of inertia which many still consider desirable for highly responsive handling.

While handling and roadholding were obviously of major concern, Fiat have not skimped on safety either. The X1/9 features a sturdy floorpan with stiff box sections at the sides and a stressed tunnel in the centre. The nose and tail sections of the body are designed to deform progressively in the event of an accident and lateral and rollover protection is provided by reinforced doors and a built in roll-hoop respectively.

With the production of soft-top cars made ever more awkward by stringent safety regulations the "Targa Top" is becoming ever more welcome. Intelligently designed in a

tough, synthetic material, that of the X1/9 is quickly removed and stows neatly under the bonnet, still leaving room for luggage in both front and rear.

But even Fiat's version of the X1/9 looks dear in terms of £ per cc. With a capacity of 1290 cc its engine is smaller than those of any of its

competitors, so despite a manly output of 73 bhp, the car tends to lag most of them in performance; this is not to say that it is slow (top speed is almost 100 mph) just that more performance can be bought for the money. Extracting more power could be a problem for in X1/9 form the 128 engine is already fairly stretched. There is no doubt the chassis could take the power, but the twin-cam engines of the 132 range will not fit.

PERFORMANCE

The lusty sohc 128 engine is a typical product of its makers. Though harsh and noisy it is graced with that rev-for-ever feel that can make Fiats fun to drive. As installed in the X1/9 it is canted forward 11 rather than 20 degrees as in the 128 saloon and employs special inlet and exhaust manifolds. Internally it benefits from lightened pistons and connecting rods as well as a higher compression ratio of 9.2:1. The outcome of these changes is an output of 73 bhp at 6000 rpm, the same as for the sporting 128 3P but 13 bhp more than that of the basic 1300 saloon; it also possesses superior torque: 71.6 lb developed at 3400 rpm.

When delivered, our test car had covered a mere 1200 miles, far too little to be giving its full performance. Accordingly we obtained a mean maximum top speed of 97.1 mph, an excellent figure for a 1300 cc car but one some eight mph short of Fiat's perhaps rather optimistic claim.

Our standing start accelerations were performed on a damp track though this seemed more of a help than a hindrance to the grippy little Fiat. Despite the wet surface it deposited a trail of rubber in its wake, shooting to 30 mph in the same time the Radbourne car took in the dry. And the car's slippery shape showed in its ability to reach close on its maximum speed before the end of the mile strip, pulling 90 mph in each direction with ease. However, the 0-60 mph acceleration time was 12.2 secs; 0.4 secs more than the Radbourne car and a full 2.2 secs down on Fiat's claim. Once again an excellent figure for a 1300 cc car and one that doubtless could be bettered after more miles, but inferior (if only slightly) to that obtained from bigger-engined rivals.

Where the lack of capacity does show up is in top gear pull, the X1/9 taking over 2.5 sec more to accelerate from 30 to 50 mph than even the 1500 cc MG Midget.

Several churns of the starter were needed to start the alloy-headed engine from cold and even making full use of the choke the warm-up period tended to be long and tedious. Even when warm, the revvy little engine suffered carburation flatspots and seemed by far its happiest on full throttle. Though thoroughly tractable at low rpm the unit does lack torque and we all found it necessary to keep the engine revving and make frequent use of the gears. With these provisos the X1/9 can be rushed along in fine style, its high cornering powers making up for its lack of power.

ECONOMY

The X1/9 is a remarkably economical sports car. Its touring consumption of 34.4 mpg demonstrates its potential, and even when subjecting the car to the enthusiastic driving it demands we still averaged in excess of 30 mpg much of the time.

With its 10.6 gallon tank the Fiat will travel up to 365 miles between fill-ups of four star fuel.

TRANSMISSION

Fiat's way of sqeezing both the engine and entire transmission into a compact space is both neat and effective. Unlike the Leyland Mini and Peugeot 104 the 128 has always had its gearbox in line with the engine. On the X1/9 the drive then passes back and down to the differential and via unequal length drive shafts to the alloy wheels.

The gearchange is controlled by a short, stubby lever ideally positioned in relation to the other major controls. However, on our car at least, its movement was neither as precise nor slick as we were expecting or remember of the Radbourne car. Following attention by the importers it improved from being intolerably baulky to having fits of non-co-operation. Most of the time the intermediate ratios would engage with a satisfying flick of the wrist. However, first was always difficult to find without a slight graunch and reverse could sometimes only be found after three or four tries. The tendency for the lever to rock with the engine was also irritating.

With 7000 revs on tap in gear, many testers had the feeling the individual ratios were on the low side. In reality this is not the case with 31, 50 and 76 mph available from the first three gears respectively. Unlike Radbourne (who fitted the lower top gear of the 128 Coupe) Fiat have retained the 0.959:1 ratio for their RHD car. As Radbourne discovered before us, this does leave a slight hole between third and top but one that rarely manifests itself. That is not to say that a five-speed gearbox wouldn't improve matters noticably.

With a pedal pressure of 25 lb the clutch is about average in weight. It proved smooth in operation and on our car at least could only have been bettered by having its take-up point further from the floor.

HANDLING

There would be little or no virtue in the X1/9's mid-engined configuration if handling and roadholding were not markedly superior to rival sports cars of conventional layout. They are, and it is the car's ability to nip through corners with kart-like agility that makes the X1/9 the fun car it is.

True to form, Fiat have employed MacPherson struts all round. At the front they are located by bottom links and brake reaction arms while at the rear wide-based, wishbones are employed. In addition there are track control arms designed to pull in the back of the outer wheel under full roll and thus counteract understeer. There is no roll bar at either end. The net result is a car that handles very nearly neutrally at all times and possesses a remarkable degree of feel. Even on extremely wet roads the comparatively light front-end hangs on tenaciously and only ham-fisted driving on slippery roads is likely to see the tail step out of line — there being insufficient power to upset it in the dry. Should understeer occur, lifting off brings the nose sharply back into line; should the tail let go it is simple enough to apply opposite lock with the accurate, precise steering. In short, though not idiot-proof the X1/9 is a remarkably safe car with excellent handling and high reserves of roadholding.

A nicely geared, sensibly-weighted rack and pinion system, the Fiat's steering is one of the best features of the car that does nothing but enhance the character of their well designed chassis. Low-profile tyres and wide-rim alloy wheels are optional equipment in Italy but included in the price on imported cars. Even with them the steering remains light but positive. The adhesion of the Pirelli P3 tyres was excellent in all conditions.

BRAKES

Good performance warrants good braking and the Fiat has a comprehensive set-up featuring discs all round and dual circuits split front to rear. There is no servo assistance, however. In practice they proved more than adequate. Round town they are light and progressive. Slowing from higher speeds reveals the lack of servo, there being a noticeable rise in pedal pressure — but there is no detectable fade, and the brakes inspire confidence from any speed.

One test they did fail was the water splash, where initially their effectiveness was practically reduced to zero. Their recovery was slow too. Another weakness that only showed at MIRA, but would affect an emergency stop, is that a deceleration of no more than 0.77g can be sustained without the front wheels locking up. This is a failing we have noted on previous X1/9s and is of course more of a worry in the wet than the dry.

The centrally mounted handbrake required a good tug to hold the car on a 1 in 3 slope but did so without difficulty. It would also effect a 0.36 retardation in an emergency.

ACCOMMODATION

Despite its wide doors the low-slung X1/9, like all modern sports cars, calls for a few contortions when getting in and out. However, even tall drivers found there was ample head, leg and shoulder room for them once installed. There is little oddment space, however, it being impossible to fit a glovebox on RHD models. Loose items therefore have to be stowed on the flat areas of the facia, in the cubbies to the side of the footwells or behind the seats — though nothing of any bulk can be put in this last space without encroaching on legroom.

In terms of luggage space the Fiat engineers have done their homework much better than most of their rivals. Apart from making provision to stow the detachable top under the bonnet they have created not one but two quite sizeable luggage compartments. The same space that houses the targa top will take up to 3.3 cu ft of luggage in an area where the battery is the only real intrusion, while the slim box behind the engine compartment will swallow a further 2.0 cu ft to give 5.3 cu ft all told. While this is still poor by absolute standards it must be considered something of a feat for a car of this size and configuration. One nice touch in imported cars is the inclusion of two special bags which allow full use to be made of this rear compartment.

Above: though non-reclining the high-back seats are extremely comfortable and the driving position generally good. Left: the basically sound instrumentation is marred by the shared grey plastic face which picks up reflections. Below left: clever packaging gives two distinct rear compartments for engine and luggage. Top right: the pedals are well laid out but the clutch is too near the steering joint. Below right: the front compartment houses luggage and the targa top. Bottom: rear boot cases are supplied with the car

Further proof of how every square inch has been utilised to the full is the way the spare wheel is stowed in its own compartment behind the driver's seat, an excellent position where it poses no limit on luggage accommodation.

RIDE COMFORT

The ride of our latest test car was better than we remember that of the earlier versions. It did not possess the characteristic low speed jiggling and would only jar on the most prominent of crevices and bumps. At higher speeds it was excellent. The superiority of the ride over that of some rivals presumably comes from Fiat's slightly different approach to suspension layout. Rather than using the stiff springs and anti-roll bars that feature on so many performance cars, they have somehow managed to endow the car with feel and good handling while employing relatively soft springing and doing without anti-roll bars altogether.

AT THE WHEEL

Not only is there sufficient room at the wheel of the X1/9 but the driving position is comfortable too. Though non-reclining, the cloth-covered seats offer support in all the vital places and all the major controls are quite well placed. Of them the pedals are the least satisfactory. Though now well-spaced for heel and toe changes they are rather tightly packed and the clutch is too close to the universal joint of the steering column — some drivers found their shoe getting caught.

The important minor controls are centred around the steering wheel, the lights master switch being positioned on the facia while the headlights and indicators are controlled by stalks mounted on the left of the column. The wash/wipe system is worked by a similar stalk on the right. The remaining facilities are controlled by rocker switches spread along the centre console, including the two-speed heater fan, the panel lights, the interior light switch, the rear screen heater, the fog lights, the hazard warning lights and a spare. Though these auxiliary controls are hardly ergonomic in layout they nevertheless fall easily to hand. Their positions are soon learnt for daytime use and their symbols are illuminated by fibre-optics at night.

VISIBILITY

Seeing out of the X1/9 is far less of a problem than with most mid-engined cars. Though low-set the seating position affords a commanding view of the nose until it finally dips out of sight and allows the stubby tail to be accurately positioned, however confined the space. Relatively slim pillars (despite the inclusion of a roll-over bar) impair rear-threequarter vision little and at no time does placing the X1/9 in traffic feel hazardous.

A door and dipping interior mirror are fitted as standard and unlike those on the Radbourne car the wipers have been changed for driving on the right. However, while they clear almost to the edge of the screen they still leave large unwiped areas at the top and bottom corners and need to be longer and more angled.

The lights of our test car were set too low and thus were not particularly effective either on main or dippped beam. Properly adjusted we reckon they would be adequate for the performance of the car. Included as standard are a pair of under-slung fog lights (which operate on dipped beam only) and a pair of automatic reversing lights.

INSTRUMENTS

We thought the comprehensive selection of well-calibrated instruments rather spoilt by their shared grey plastic face with its yellow lines. More important, however, are the reflections of the facia which appear in the one-piece glass and tend to distract the driver's attention.

In use, the selection of rectangular and round dials proved pleasingly accurate and the combination of fuel, water, temperature and oil pressure gauges together with speedometer and rev-counter was quite sufficient to keep the driver fully informed.

Night time illumination is controlled by a two-position switch on the console and is most effective. Unfortunately it also causes severe reflections in the windscreen.

HEATING

The heater unit is traditional Fiat with a trap door at its base for controlling distribution. However, on the X1/9 its opening and closing is controlled by a vertical central lever in a group of three. The level on its left determines the quantity of fresh air entering the passenger compartment and that on its right the temperature. As always with Fiats the annotation could have proved confusing had we not seen it before. We found the heat slow to come through and the flow only moderate even when using the fast speed of the blower.

VENTILATION

There are a total of four vents in the X1/9, two on centre console and one at

MOTOR ROAD TEST NO 13/77 • FIAT X1/9

PERFORMANCE

CONDITIONS

Weather	Damp: wind 0-5 mph
Temperature	39°F
Barometer	29.05 in Hg
Surface	Damp tarmac

MAXIMUM SPEEDS

	mph	kph
Banked Circuit	97.1	156.2
Best ¼ mile	97.8	157.3
Terminal Speeds:		
at ¼ mile	72	116
at kilometre	87	140
at mile	93	150
Speed in gears (at 7000 rpm):		
1st	31	50
2nd	50	80
3rd	76	122

ACCELERATION FROM REST

mph	sec	kph	sec
0-30	3.7	0-40	2.7
0-40	5.6	0-60	5.0
0-50	8.5	0-80	8.4
0-60	12.2	0-100	13.0
0-70	16.7	0-120	20.4
0-80	25.1	0-140	35.4
0-90	40.7		
Stand'g ¼	18.1	Stand'g km	34.9

ACCELERATION IN TOP

mph	sec	kph	sec
20-40	12.1	40-60	7.2
30-50	11.2	60-80	7.2
40-60	12.4	80-100	8.2
50-70	13.9	100-120	9.8
60-80	16.8	120-140	16.1

FUEL CONSUMPTION

Touring*	34.4 mpg
	8.2 litres/100 km

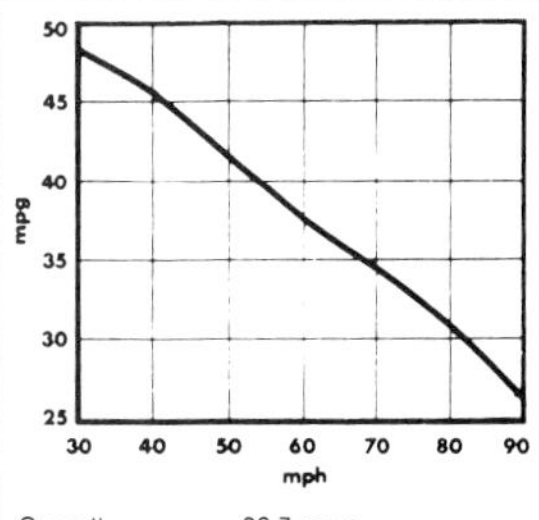

Overall	29.7 mpg
	9.5 litres/100 km
Fuel grade	98 octane
	4 star rating
Tank capacity	10.6 galls
	48.2 litres
Max range	364.6 miles
	586.6 km
Test distance	1002 miles
	1612 km

*Consumption midway between 30 mph and maximum less 5 per cent for acceleration

BRAKES

Pedal pressure deceleration and stopping distance from 30 mph (48 kph)

lb	kg	g	ft	m
25	11	0.25	120	37
50	23	0.53	57	17
75	34	0.77	49	12
Handbrake		0.36	83	25

FADE

20½g stops at 1 min intervals from speed midway between 40 mph (64 kph) and maximum (68.5 mph, 110.2 kph)

	lb	kg
Pedal force at start	48	19
Pedal force at 10th stop	50	20
Pedal force at 20th stop	50	20

STEERING

Turning circle between kerbs

	ft	m
left	30.3	9.2
right	32.9	10.0
lock to lock	3.1 turns	
50ft diam. circle	0.8 turns	

CLUTCH

	in	cm
Free pedal movement	1.0	2.5
Additional to disengage	3.5	8.9
Maximum pedal load	25lb	11.4 kg

SPEEDOMETER (mph)

Speedo						
30	40	50	60	70	80	90
True mph						
30	40	50	60	69.5	79.5	90

Distance recorder: accurate

WEIGHT

	cwt	kg
Unladen weight*	16.7	848.4
Weight as tested	20.4	1036.3

*with fuel for approx 50 miles

Performance tests carried out by Motor's staff at the Motor Industry Research Association proving ground, Lindley.

GENERAL SPECIFICATION

ENGINE

Cylinders	4 in line
Capacity	1290 cc (78.66 cu in)
Bore/stroke	86/55.5 mm (3.39/2.19 in)
Cooling	Water
Block	Cast iron
Head	Aluminium alloy
Valves	Sohc
Valve timing	
inlet opens	24° btdc
inlet closes	68 abdc
ex opens	64° bbdc
ex closes	28° atdc
Compression	9.2:1
Carburettor	Weber twin choke 32 DMTR 22
Bearings	5 main
Fuel pump	Mechanical
Max power	73 bhp (DIN) at 6000 rpm
Max torque	71.6 lb ft (DIN) at 3400 rpm

TRANSMISSION

Type	4 speed manual
Clutch	7.25 in dia, sdp, diaphragm spring
Internal ratios and mph/1000 rpm	
Top	0.959:1/16.6
3rd	1.454:1/10.9
2nd	2.235:1/7.1
1st	3.580:1/4.4
Rev	3.714:1
Final drive	4.076:1

BODY/CHASSIS

Construction	Unitary, all steel with detachable roof
Protection	Body panels fully rust treated during construction. Secondary treatment applied in the UK

SUSPENSION

Front	Ind. by MacPherson structs, transverse links, brake reaction arms and coils
Rear	Ind. by MacPherson struts, lower wishbones, track control arms and coils

STEERING

Type	Rack and pinion
Assistance	None
Toe in	0.118 mm
Camber	−0°
Castor	7°
Rear toe in	0.394 in

BRAKES

Type	Discs all round
Servo	No
Circuit	Dual, front/rear
Rear valve	No
Adjustment	Automatic

WHEELS

Type	Aluminium alloy 5J × 13
Tyres	165/70 SR 13
Pressures	26 psi front; 29 psi rear

ELECTRICAL

Battery	12V, 45Ah
Polarity	Negative earth
Generator	Alternator
Fuses	12
Headlights	2× 45/40 watt

IN SERVICE

GUARANTEE

Duration ... **6 months, unlimited mileage**

MAINTENANCE

Schedule	**Every 6000 miles**
Free service	**at 1500 miles**
Labour for year	**7.5 hours**

DO-IT-YOURSELF

Sump	**7.5 pints, 20W50**
Transmission	**5.3 pints, SAE 90**
Coolant	**19.3 pints**
Chassis lubrication	**None**
Contact breaker gap	**0.40 mm**
Spark plug type	**Champion N7Y**
Spark plug gap	**0.5-0.6 mm**
Tappets (cold)	**inlet 0.4 mm**
	exhaust 0.45 mm

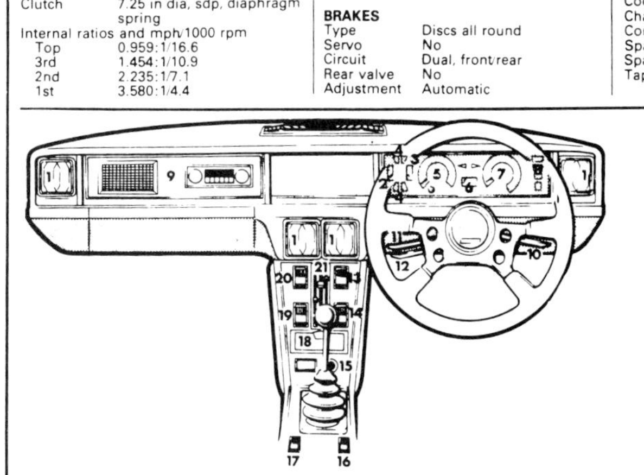

1 face level vents
2 oil pressure gauge
3 water temperature gauge
4 warning lights
5 speedometer
6 fuel gauge
7 rev-counter
8 warning lights
9 radio
10 wash/wipe
11 head light control
12 indicators
13 fog lights
14 interior light
15 cigar lighter
16 spare
17 heated rear window
18 ashtray
19 instrument lights
20 heater boost
21 heater controls

Make: Fiat **Model**: X1/9 "special"
Maker: S.A. Fiat Corso G. Agnelli 200, Turin, Italy
Concessionaires: Fiat (England) Ltd, Great West Road, Brentford, Middx
Price: £2562.00 plus £213.50 car tax plus £222.04 VAT and seat belts at £29.50 gives total as tested of £3027.04

Star rating guide

either end of the facia. The central ones distribute air from the heater and are fan boostable. Those on the outside, however, draw in cold air and rely entirely on ram pressure. Though not particularly powerful at town speeds they provide a good throughput of cold air from 30 mph onward. Though only adjustable in the vertical plane the flaps also allow quite accurate aiming.

NOISE

★★★ Unlike the Radbourne car our latest X1/9 proved to be uncomfortably noisy. While one perhaps expects, and will tolerate, a degree of rortiness in a fun car we felt the levels of both wind and engine noise were unacceptable by modern standards. Fiat engines tend to be harsh and noisy and this version of the 128 unit is no exception; while mellow up to around 3500-4000 rpm the note becomes altogether more obtrusive from there up to 7000 rpm, where it is extemely loud by any standards. Wind noise was far more perceptible than on the Radbourne car and emanated from around the leading edges of the doors and towards the rear of the targa top. There was a noticeable degree of whine in the intermediates and very perceptible idler rattle from the transmission at tickover. Road noise is well suppressed.

FINISH

★★★ Produced by Bertone in Turin, the X1/9 is an example of the pros and cons of cars built by coachbuilders. For instance the doors sounded tinny when closing, the engine cover drips water all down the side of the engine and the facia and console are more typical of a "special" than most other production cars. On the other hand all the panels fitted well, the pop-up lights worked extremely efficienctly and there were nice little touches like the neatly recessed releases for engine and rear compartment (though they are on the wrong side for the UK), and neat stowage of the spare wheel. The metallic paintwork (standard on imported cars) was well finished and the interior trim quite plush, though the striped "deck-chair" seat covers were not to everyone's taste.

EQUIPMENT

★★★★ As sold in the UK the X1/9 is well equipped by any standards. Undoubtedly its biggest asset over the new tin-top brigade is the detachable roof. Light but strong it is easily detached and stowed and will doubtless alone account for many X1/9 sales. In addition the car comes with low-profile tyres on alloy rims, fitted suitcases, fog lights, a heated rear window, door mirror, cigar lighter, tinted glass, built-in head restraints, a rev-counter and a radio.

When we tested the car the radio was a prototype installation and was not up to standard. Customer cars should be better in this respect. Short of a clock we could see no obvious omissions in the comprehensive specification.

IN SERVICE

While it may look rather unique to the uninitiated, the X1/9 should cause few if any problems with servicing, as most of its components are from the 128.

Though the engine is a tight squeeze in its central compartment most items are reasonably accessible. Even the distributor is not out of reach.

Items not found in the engine compartment include the fuses, which are under the facia, the battery and reservoirs which are in the front compartment and the spare wheel which is behind the driver's seat.

Servicing is required every 6000 miles. The free service is at 1500 miles. The guarantee lasts for six months of unlimited mileage.

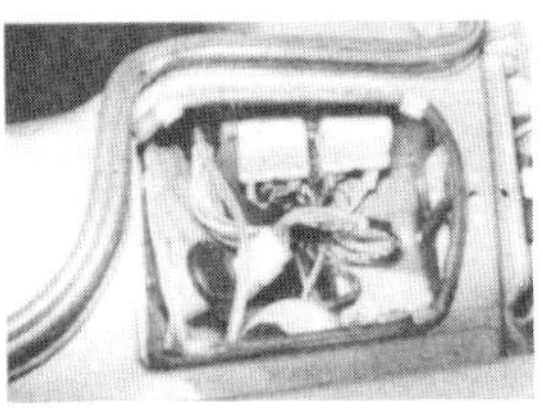

Above: neatly installed in the offside wing are the washer bottle and headlamp relays. Below: the pop-up lights work well. The fog lights are standard too. Below right: as fitted by Fiat the excellent Toric belts hamper spare wheel removal

The Rivals

FIAT X1/9 £2998

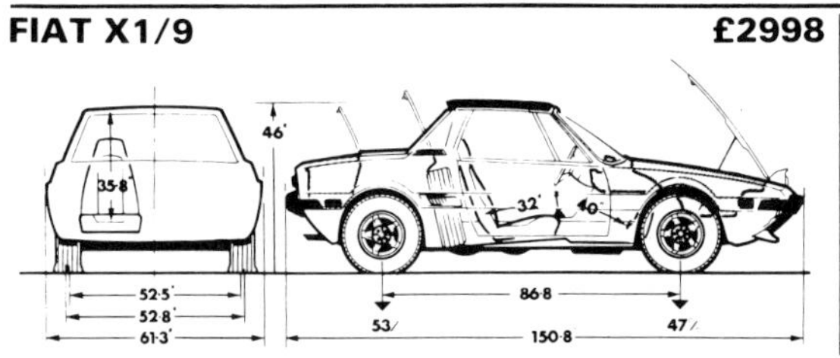

LOTUS EUROPA SPECIAL £3225 (S/H)

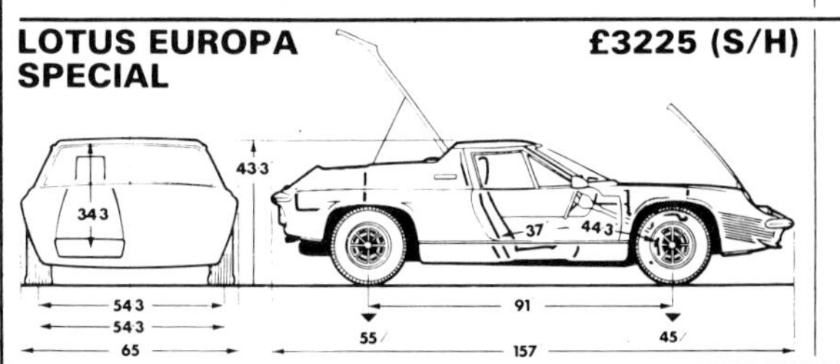

MG MIDGET £2085

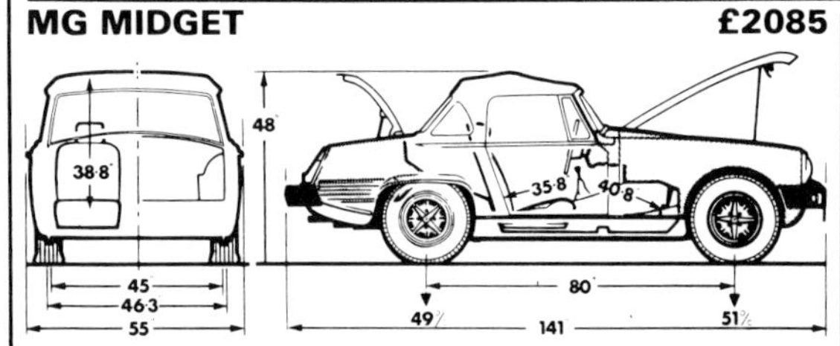

MGB £2843

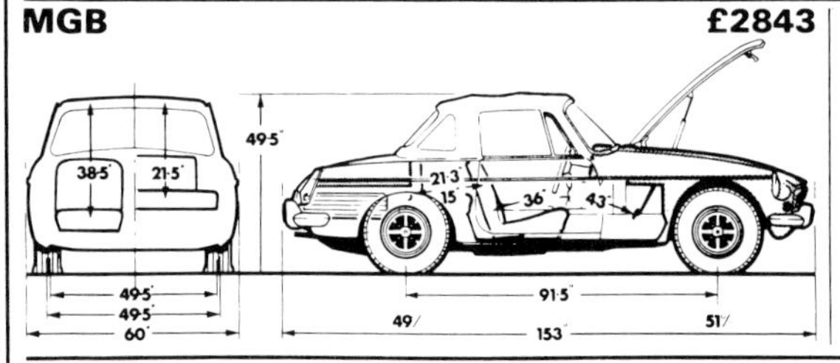

TRIUMPH SPITFIRE £2359

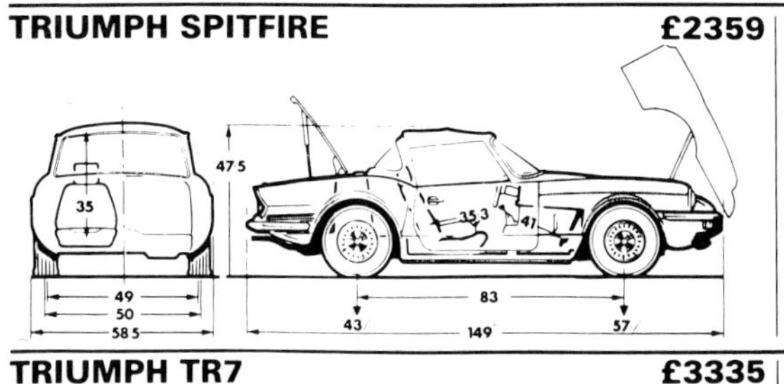

TRIUMPH TR7 £3335

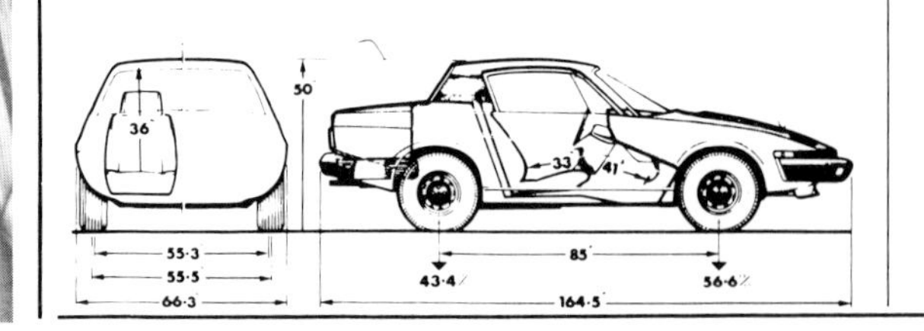

Apart from our ageing selection of rag tops the X1/9 has few rivals other than the TR7; hence we have included a second-hand Europa in our charts. Other such competitors would be the TR6 and Lotus Elan

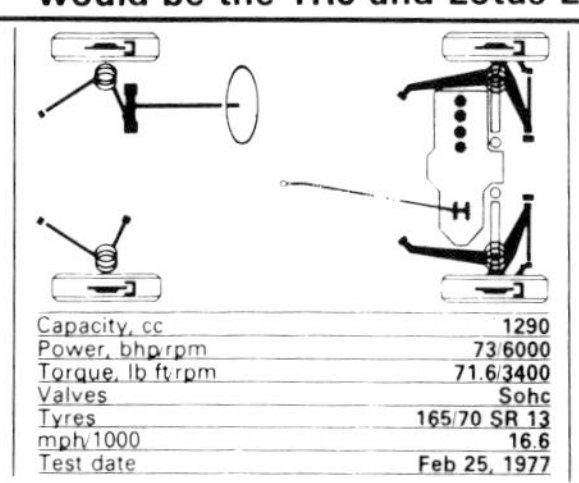

Capacity, cc	1290
Power, bhp/rpm	73/6000
Torque, lb ft/rpm	71.6/3400
Valves	Sohc
Tyres	165/70 SR 13
mph/1000	16.6
Test date	Feb 25, 1977

Recently introduced into the UK in "Special" form complete with plush interior, tinted glass, radio, alloy wheels etc. A fun car with superb handling and roadholding and gutsy, economical 1300 cc engine. Facility of excellent targa top. Despite its lively performance could handle still more power. The gearchange is inconsistent and the car suffers from high engine and wind noise.

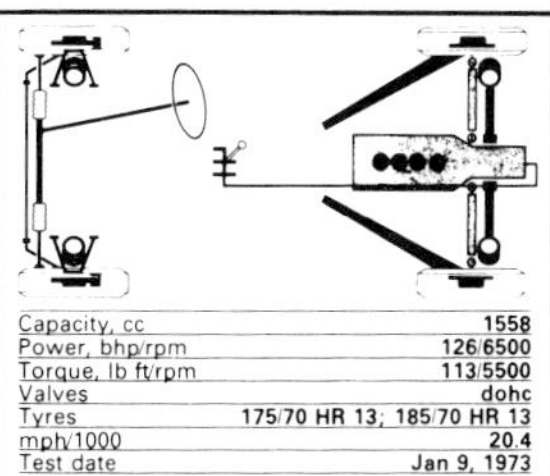

Capacity, cc	1558
Power, bhp/rpm	126/6500
Torque, lb ft/rpm	113/5500
Valves	dohc
Tyres	175/70 HR 13; 185/70 HR 13
mph/1000	20.4
Test date	Jan 9, 1973

Sadly no longer in production but a strong rival even in second-hand form (our price is for a 1975 one). The only one of the sextet to match and indeed surpass the Fiat on handling. Astonishing performance from light, aerodynamic body powered by potent twin-cam engine. Finish inconsistent, but a fine looking car that will turn heads for many years to come. A relaxed high-speed cruiser with excellent ride.

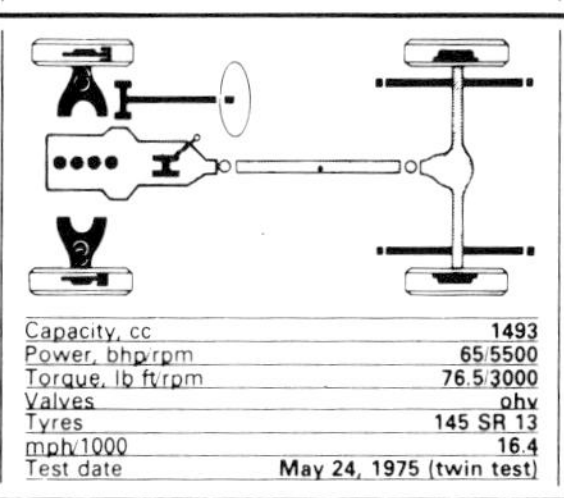

Capacity, cc	1493
Power, bhp/rpm	65/5500
Torque, lb ft/rpm	76.5/3000
Valves	ohv
Tyres	145 SR 13
mph/1000	16.4
Test date	May 24, 1975 (twin test)

One of Leyland's old timers. Still a great fun car but one changed by legislation rather than the search for improvement. Now fitted with strangled version of Triumph 1500 engine rather than the ubiquitous "A" series. Handling still incredibly controllable but neither it nor (poor) roadholding improved by new federal ride height. Betters the opposition hands down on price while providing economical, wind-in-the hair motoring.

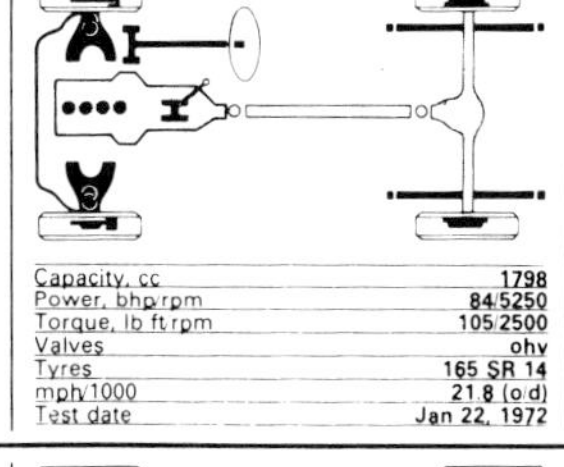

Capacity, cc	1798
Power, bhp/rpm	84/5250
Torque, lb ft/rpm	105/2500
Valves	ohv
Tyres	165 SR 14
mph/1000	21.8 (o/d)
Test date	Jan 22, 1972

The other old man of the Leyland stable. Laughed at by some for its ageing, heavy body and cramped unergonomic interior but still selling well to those who appreciate reliable, soft-top motoring. "B" series engine provides low output for capacity but is relatively economical, astonishingly rugged and cheap to repair. Like Midget, has been altered to meet legislation, losing power and roadholding in the process. Clean secondhand ones very sought after.

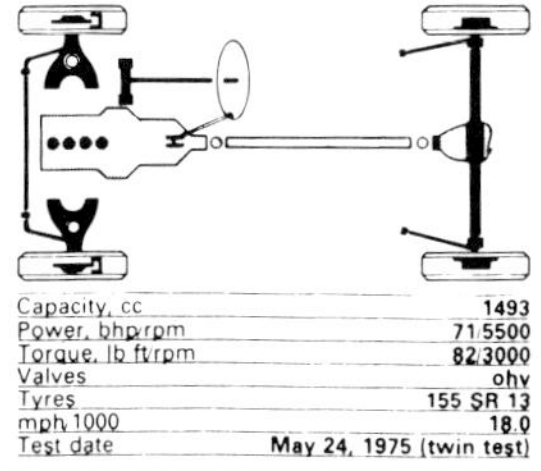

Capacity, cc	1493
Power, bhp/rpm	71/5500
Torque, lb ft/rpm	82/3000
Valves	ohv
Tyres	155 SR 13
mph/1000	18.0
Test date	May 24, 1975 (twin test)

Yet another of Leyland's soft-top fleet which uses same engine as Midget. Handling used to be its Achilles Heel but has been steadily improved over the years. Particularly good points are its diminutive turning circle and its exceptionally accessible underbonnet area. A lighter body and apparently better aerodynamics grace the car with slightly better performance and appreciably better economy than the Midget. It is also quieter and prettier to most eyes.

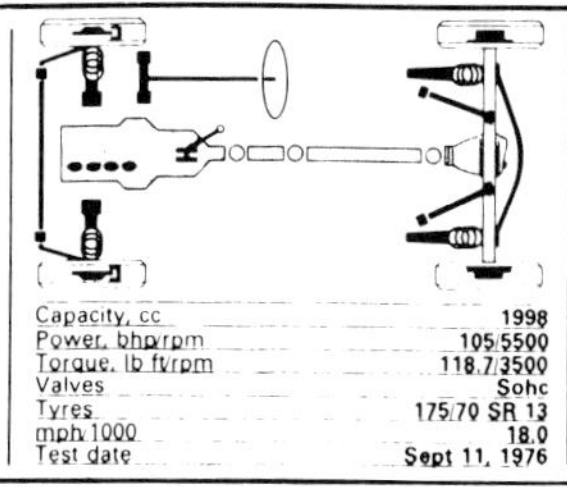

Capacity, cc	1998
Power, bhp/rpm	105/5500
Torque, lb ft/rpm	118.7/3500
Valves	Sohc
Tyres	175/70 SR 13
mph/1000	18.0
Test date	Sept 11, 1976

The new generation Leyland two-seater with modern wedge-shaped styling but conventional layout with front-mounted Dolomite engine driving the rear wheels. Early cars suffered from poor quality control, but good ones are fun to drive with adequate performance and ride/handling compromise. Too noisy by modern standards and suffers from poor vision. Plus points include plush interior, good instrumentation, heating and ventilation.

Comparisons

PERFORMANCE	Fiat	Lotus Europa S/H	MG Midget	MGB	Triumph Spitfire	Triumph TR7
Max speed, mph	97.1	121.7	96.5	106.2	98.5	111.2
Max in 4th	—	96	—	—	—	—
3rd	76	72	70	75	77	94
2nd	50	49	47	49	50	66
1st	31	32	29	31	31	44
0-60 mph, secs	12.2	6.6	11.9	11.5	11.8	9.6
30-50 mph in 4th, secs	11.2	6.3	8.6	9.3	9.3	7.5
50-70 mph in top, secs	13.9	11.5	9.4	10.5	10.7	7.8
Weights, cwt	16.7	14.0	16.4	19.6	15.5	19.3
Turning circle, ft*	31.6	36.7	31.8	30.9	21.3	27.8
50ft circle, turns	0.8	0.8	0.7	0.9	0.75	1.05
Boot capacity, cu.ft.	5.3	4.8	†3.1	†4.4	†5.6	7.7

*mean of left and right †measured with boxes not cases

COSTS	Fiat	Lotus Europa S/H	MG Midget	MGB	Triumph Spitfire	Triumph TR7
Price, inc VAT & tax, £	2998	3225	2085	2843	2359	3335
Insurance group	6	7	5	6	5	6
Overall mpg	29.7	24.2	27.3	23.5	29.8	28.0
Touring mpg	34.4	33.1	29.0	29.0	35.4	31.4
Fuel grade (stars)	4	4	4	4	4	4
Tank capacity, gals	10.6	12.5	7.0	12.0	7.3	12.0
Service interval, miles	6000	5000	6000	6000	6000	6000
Front brake pads £*	4.86	8.42	6.93	7.76	6.15	11.43
Oil filter, £*	2.29	2.45	2.08	1.38	2.86	1.24
Starter Motor, £*	25.37	62.04	11.23	51.72	11.23	28.04
Windscreen, £*	†	63.37**	8.58	20.52**	13.93	33.48

*inc VAT **Laminated †to be decided

EQUIPMENT	Fiat	Lotus Europa S/H	MG Midget	MGB	Triumph Spitfire	Triumph TR7
Adjustable steering						
Carpets	●	●	●	●	●	●
Central locking						
Cigar lighter	●			●		●
Clock				●		●
Cloth trim	●	●		●		
Dipping mirror	●	●	●	●	●	●
Dual circuit brakes	●		●	●	●	●
Electric windows		●				
Fresh air vents	●	●		●		●
Hazard flashers	●		●	●	●	●
Headlamp washers						
Head restraints	●	●	●	●	●	●
Heated rear window	●					●
Laminated screen		●		●	●	●
Locker				●	●	●
Outside mirror	●	●	●	●	●	●
Petrol filler lock						
Radio	●					
Rear central armrest						
Rear wash/wipe						
Rev counter	●	●	●	●	●	●
Seat belts — front		●	●	●	●	●
rear						
Seat recline			●	●	●	●
Sliding roof						
Tinted glass	●					
Windscreen wash/wipe	●			●	●	●
Wiper delay					●	

Conclusions

THOUGH expensive for a 1300 cc car, the well-equipped X1/9 will doubtless find its own niche in the UK market. It is stylish, fun to drive, economical and next to our own ageing rag tops is about the nearest you can get to real wind-in-the hair motoring at the price.

Though small in overall dimensions it is a roomy package thanks to very clever utilisation of space. It is also an extremely well balanced car with exceptionally responsive handling and very acceptable roadholding. With the production of soft tops being made ever more awkward by safety legislation the targa top sports car would seem to be the way to go, and of existing designs we would regard the X1/9 as outstanding.

Where it disappoints is in general refinement. The doors close with a tinny clang, the considerable wind noise suggests a bad fitting targa top and poor seals, and engine noise is not well suppressed. Though extremely lively for its capacity the engine does lack torque. What a car it would be with a bigger engine, though!

It is far more stylish and better handling than either the Midget or Spitfire and it is certainly more agile and economical than the MGB. Its closest rival, despite its tin roof, is Leyland's TR7 and the choice there will depend on priorities, though the X1/9 is more our idea of a sports car.

Road Test

FIAT X1/9 1500

Ever since the X1/9 was first introduced it's been crying out for a bigger engine and a five-speed gearbox to make the most of its outstanding handling and roadholding — and now its got them. Does it live up to expectations?

BRITISH SPORTS car buyers had to wait an inordinately long while — four years — before the delightful Berton-styled X1/9 finally became available on the UK market in early 1977, but Fiat did at least partly make amends by choosing the UK to launch the new and much pleaded for 1500cc version, which made its world debut at the NEC Motor Show last October.

Ever since the original 1972 launch of this baby mid-engined exoticar, which is based on the mechanical components of the 128 saloon, it was clear that the X1/9's remarkable agility and roadholding deserved a much higher performance than was provided by its uprated 1290cc engine. As we said in our February 1977 road test, "What a car it would be with a bigger engine, though!"

But it wasn't until April last year, when Fiat launched the Ritmo saloon, that a bigger-capacity version of this basic unit became available in Fiat's parts bins; top versions of the Ritmo have a stroked 1498cc version mated to a five-speed gearbox, and it is this power pack which has now, predictably enough, become available in the little sportster.

At the same time the X1/9 1500 incorporates a number of other changes, the most apparent being the US spec 5 mph impact resistant bumpers which increase overall length by some five inches. The engine cover is higher to accommodate the taller engine, while inside there are new instruments, a redesigned facia, and re-upholstered seats.

Apart from the engine and gearbox, the X1/9 is mechanically unchanged, retaining its all round independent suspension by MacPherson struts, and disc brakes on all four wheels.

At £4575 the X1/9 1500 is not

particularly cheap, but its sophisticated layout and specification make its (mostly cheaper) rivals look distinctly crude and old-fashioned in comparison; cars like the MGB roadster (£3996) and Midget (£2971) are conventionally laid out with front-mounted engines and live rear axles; the Spitfire (£3365) at least has independent suspension but it, too, has an antiquated pushrod engine, while the TR7 (£4764) is not yet available with a detachable roof and is also conventionally engineered. Another car that could be considered as a rival — at any rate if bought only for leisure use — is the shatteringly fast but uncivilised £4,134 Caterham Super 7 Twin Cam.

As installed in the X1/9 the alloy-head engine has been uprated to produce 85 bhp (DIN) at 6000 rpm, 12 bhp more than the superseded 1300, while torque is increased by over 20 per cent to 87 lb ft at 3200 rpm. In spite of an increase in stroke, from 55.5 mm to 63.9 mm, the engine still has substantially over-square cylinder dimensions with its 86 mm bore. This, plus a single overhead camshaft, five-bearing crankshaft, and twin-choke Weber carburetter, adds up to a tough and revvy little engine which will go to 6900 rpm.

The transformation wrought by the bigger engine and five-speed gearbox is even greater than we expected. Our test car romped from 0 to 60 mph in just 9.9 sec, 2.3 sec faster than the old 1300. Higher up the speed range the difference is even more marked, the 0-90 mph time coming down from 40.7 sec to 25.4 sec; and the top speed is increased by over 10 mph, from 97.1 to 107.7 mph.

Even in its higher-geared fifth speed the 1500 accelerates faster than the 1300 did in top; the 30-50 mph time is reduced from 11.2 to 10.0 sec, 50-70 mph is down from 13.9 sec to 11.0 sec, and so on up the speed range. And in fourth gear the little Fiat is now a match, at least up to about 50 mph, for even the 2-litre TR7, with a 30-50 mph time, for example, of just 7.4 sec.

In fact, in most other aspects of its performance, too, the X1/9 is now snapping at the heels of the TR7, and it can now show a clean pair of heels to BL's other sportsters, the 1,800 cc MGB and the 1,500 cc Midget and Spitfire. At last, and in no uncertain manner, the X1/9 has the outright performance that its chassis and its appearance deserve.

It's not all plaudits, however, for although the increase in stroke has not diminished the sheer zest, nor the astonishing smoothness with which this tough little unit revs to almost 7000 rpm, it also remains very noisy when driven hard. And although engine noise is not necessarily undesirable in a sports car, that of the X1/9 has a harsh and rather "tinny" quality that few of our testers liked. Cruising at between 60 and 75 mph is marred by a boom period, and though cruising in the high 80s is smooth and unstrained, it is far from quiet. Indeed, the *car* feels able to maintain cruising speeds as high as 100 mph — a speed which comes up easily even on quite short straights — but the consequent noise levels are higher than most people will want to bear.

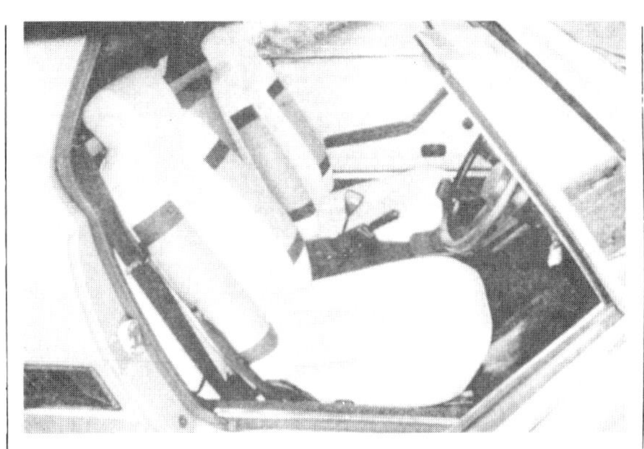

Above: most of our testers thought the new seats — with cloth inserts in the side bolsters — to be a change for the worse, though they are still reasonably comfortable

Left: legroom seems to have suffered, but otherwise the driving position is good, not Italianate in any way. Note the new locker, relocated heater controls, and new instruments, below

Another irritation is that, while the increased low speed torque is unmistakeable and very welcome, half the benefit is off-set by annoying part-throttle hesitations below 2500 rpm, which are aggravated by a jerky accelerator action. And while the automatic choke ensures fairly prompt starting from cold, warm-up is slow and plagued by carburation flat-spots.

These snags suggest very weak jetting of the carburetters primary choke, an assumption supported by the excellent fuel consumption figures we recorded at MIRA, which are consistently better than the old car's. The steady speed fuel consumption does not drop below 40 mpg until 60 mph is reached, and you have to be doing well over 80 mph to do less than 30 mpg. Even at a steady 100 mph the X1/9 is doing almost 23 mpg. The result of these figures is a 34 mpg computed touring consumption that is only marginally heavier than the old car's 34.4 mpg, in spite of the 1500's much higher top speed. Similarly, the overall consumption, despite all the extra weight and performance, is only a little worse: 29.0 mpg compared to 29.7 mpg. Most private owners should expect to average well over 30 mpg and have a range of around 350 miles per 10.6 gallon tankful of four star fuel.

The five-speed gearbox retains the same well-spaced first, second and third gear ratios as before, giving 30, 49 and 75 mph respectively at the 6900 rpm limit. Fourth gear is now lower, thereby answering our previous complaint of a slight "hole" between third and fourth, while fifth provides a semi-overdrive ratio giving 18.3 mph per 1000 rpm, compared to 16.6 mph per 1000 rpm in top for the four-speed box.

Most of our testers also felt the gearchange was much improved, enabling very quick and easy changes once the spring bias to the 3rd/4th plane has been mastered, though to get the best out of it you do need to use *full* travel of the heavyish but smooth-acting clutch.

The X1/9's steering is still as light, as quick, and as precise as ever, but in other respects we were a little disappointed with our test car: there is very little self-centring, so that it feels dead around the straight-ahead position, and in the freezing conditions that prevailed during part of our test we were disconcerted to find that even on lock the steering provided very little information about the state of the road surface. Since we can recall no such problems with previous X1/9s we can only assume — and hope — that our barely run-in test car's steering rack still required some loosening up.

Otherwise the X1/9's excellent roadholding on wet and dry roads, and its go-where-you-point it agility, are as before, with a balance that is to all intents and purposes neutral up to very high cornering speeds. Eventually it will start to understeer, while lifting off causes quite sharp tuck-in — or even oversteer if you're going fast enough — but not too viciously for a competent driver to catch it with a twitch of opposite lock. And although feel through the steering of our test car was disappointing, there is plenty of advance warning "through the seat of your pants" before the Pirelli P3s finally lose adhesion. Less satisfactory aspect of the handling is the poor directional stability at high cruising speed.

When we first tested an X1/9 at MIRA in 1977 we found that maximum stopping power was limited — to a poor 0.77g deceleration — by the front wheels locking. We did not repeat those tests on the latest car, but could find no fault with its braking on the road; even hard braking on a wet road can be accomplished without premature front wheel lock-up (unlike some mid-engined cars) while pedal weight and progression are almost perfect. At no time was even a hint of brake fade encountered.

The X1/9 is no longer supplied with custom-made cases for its rear boot, but otherwise the surprisingly generous (for the type of car) luggage accommodation is as before, with front and rear compartments that between them accommodated 5.3 cu ft of our rigid test luggage; with soft bags, there should be room for a fair bit more. New to the 1500 version is a glove locker on the passenger side of the facia.

Passenger accommodation can only be described as fair; you would not have to be unusually tall to want for more legroom; and with the seat well back, the proximity of the rear bulkhead limits the rake of the backrest if you like a semi-reclining posture. Although none of our testers was particularly *un*comfortable at the wheel — the major controls are well laid out and the seat quite comfortable — there were a number of minor complaints; that the throttle pedal was too close and awkwardly angled; that the seat backrest was a bit narrow for broad-shouldered drivers; that the gear-lever is placed a little too far back for those who like or need to sit close to the wheel; and that your toes can touch the lower steering column when operating the clutch. But these are comments, rather than serious criticisms.

Column stalks are to Fiat's usual pattern, with a single right hand one for the wash/wipe system, and two on the left catering for headlamp beam and indicators respectively. Other minor controls are strange, gimmicky Ritmo-style rocker switches on the facia and centre console, where their positions are soon learned.

Thankfully, Fiat has avoided any gimmickry in the presentation of the new instruments. As before they are all under a single pane of glass (which is not entirely successful in banishing reflections), with large round dials for tachometer and speedometer in front of the driver, and the fuel gauge between them. A third round housing to the left is segmented for oil pressure and water temperature gauges, which tend to

continued over

Left: two lids at the rear, for the mid-mounted engine and for the rear luggage compartment; the release catches are mounted on the nearside rear door pillar

Left: front compartment houses fluid reservoirs and stores the Targa roof panel when it is detached — and takes a useful amount of luggage

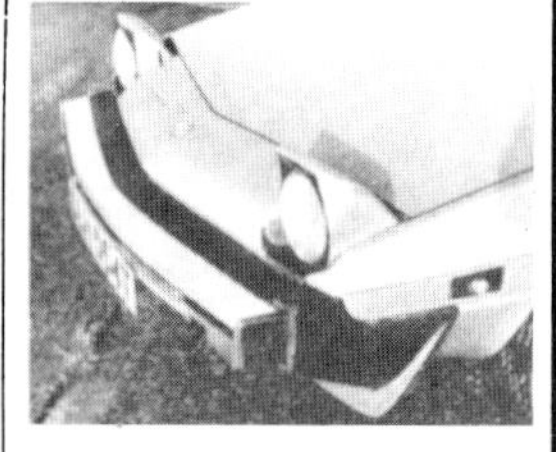

Below: note large new bumpers and pop-up lights

be obscured from view by the wheel. All the gauges are comprehensively and crisply calibrated. The clock is now a sensibly situated L.E.D. digital unit.

Though now relocated higher up on the facia, the heater's basic controls are as before with three sliders controlling distribution, air volume, and temperature respectively, and a two speed booster fan. Maximum temperature is adequate and heated air can be obtained to the screen, or footwells, or through the two vents on the centre console. We found it very difficult to adjust the temperature effectively as the control is very unprogressive in action.

With the heater off, fan-boosted fresh air is available through the centre console vents, otherwise fresh air is available, on ram effect only, through the face-level vents at either end of the facia. Flow is modest at town speeds, reasonable at higher speeds, but the vents are so located that the cold air tends to freeze the driver's right hand if aimed towards his face.

For a small sports car, the X1/9 provides a reasonably comfortable ride. It is distinctly firm and jiggly at low speeds, but not unacceptably so, and at higher speeds improves quite markedly. Firm damping and very moderate body roll mean peace of mind for passengers, even at high cornering speeds.

Bump thump and tyre roar are both quite well suppressed, and wind noise, though ever-present, is really quite low for a car with a detachable lid; a whistle becomes apparent at about 90 mph, but at lower speeds there is little problem — largely because engine noise dominates. Although the engine does not sound strained at peak revs in the gears or even at very high cruising speeds, it does pass through a number of boom periods — which are particularly pronounced on the overrun — and overall noise volume is such that you may as well switch off the radio when motoring fast. There is, additionally, a very high pitched whine from the gears — somewhat reminiscent of a Ferrari Dino!

Not everyone thought the new vinyl upholstery, which has replaced the previous striped cloth, to be a step in the right direction, but otherwise the finish was considered reasonably neat and tasteful. The car feels less tinny than it used to, though there are still a few irritating squeaks and rattles, and some wires can be seen hanging loose under the facia.

The X1/9 is adequately rather than exceptionally well equipped; it no longer comes with fitted cases nor a radio as standard, though it has gained a digital clock, a locker, and seat recline. Other items of note are alloy wheels and tinted glass.

Unlike most other Fiats, the X1/9's wash/wipe system incorporates *two* constant wiper speeds in addition to intermittent wipe, but a serious failing is the blind spot created in dirty weather by a wide unswept area at the right of the screen. We found the headlights rather feeble whether on dip or main beam, and it is not possible to drive with sidelights on only; either you have no lights at all, or you have to have the lot, with the headlamps up and creating extra drag which must have a detrimental effect on mpg at motorway speeds.

As mid-engined cars go, the X1/9 is very easy to see out of on the move, but when parking, you do need to remember the extra length of the 5-mph bumpers which protrude a long way and are invisible from the driver's seat.

MOTOR ROAD TEST NO 4/79 ●
FIAT X1/9 1500

PERFORMANCE

CONDITIONS

Weather	Wind 0-15 mph
Temperature	33-38°F
Barometer	29.5 in Hg
Surface	Damp tarmacadam

MAXIMUM SPEEDS

	mph	kph
Banked Circuit	107.7	172.3
Best ¼ mile	111.1	178.8
Terminal Speeds:		
at ¼ mile	78	126
at kilometre	96	154
at mile	102	164
Speed in gears (at 6900 rpm):		
1st	30	48
2nd	49	79
3rd	75	121
4th	105	169

ACCELERATION FROM REST

mph	sec	kph	sec
0-30	3.1	0-40	2.3
0-40	4.7	0-60	4.2
0-50	7.1	0-80	7.1
0-60	9.9	0-100	10.5
0-70	13.2	0-120	15.0
0-80	18.3	0-140	23.0
0-90	25.4		
Stand'g ¼	17.2	Stand'g km	32.3

ACCELERATION IN TOP

mph	sec	kph	sec
20-40	10.3	40-60	6.3
30-50	10.0	60-80	6.3
40-60	10.6	80-100	6.7
50-70	11.0	100-120	7.6
60-80	12.8	120-140	10.1
70-90	16.6		

ACCELERATION IN 4TH

mph	sec	kph	sec
20-40	7.6	40-60	4.6
30-50	7.4	60-80	4.6
40-60	7.8	80-100	5.1
50-70	8.4	100-120	5.5
60-80	9.4	120-140	7.8
70-90	12.5		

FUEL CONSUMPTION

Touring*	34.0 mpg 8.3 litres/100 km
Overall	29.0 mpg 9.7 litres/100 km
Govt tests	26.6 mpg (urban) 47.2 mpg (56 mph) 36.8 mpg (75 mph)
Fuel grade	97 octane 4 star rating
Tank capacity	10.6 galls 48 litres
Max range	360 miles 579 km
Test distance	1170 miles 1883 km

*Consumption midway between 30 mph and maximum less 5 per cent for acceleration.

SPEEDOMETER (mph)

Speedo	30	40	50	60	70	80	90	100
True mph	29	39	49	59	68	78	88	98

Distance recorder. 3 per cent fast

WEIGHT

	cwt	kg
Unladen weight*	18.0	914
Weight as tested	21.7	1102

*with fuel for approx 50 miles

Performance tests carried out at 400 miles by Motor's staff at the Motor Industry Research Association proving ground, Lindley.

GENERAL SPECIFICATION

ENGINE

Cylinders	4 transverse, mid-mounted
Capacity	1498 cc (91.4 cu in)
Bore/stroke	86.4/63.9 mm (3.4/2.5 in)
Cooling	Water
Block	Cast Iron
Head	Alloy
Valves	Sohc
Cam drive	Belt
Valve timing	
inlet opens	24° btdc
inlet closes	68° abdc
ex opens	64° bbdc
ex closes	28° atdc
Compression	9.2:1
Carburetter	Weber 34 DATR twin-choke downdraught
Bearings	5 main
Max power	85 bhp (DIN) at 6000 rpm
Max torque	86.8 lb ft (DIN) at 3200 rpm

TRANSMISSION

Type	5-speed manual
Clutch dia	7.5 in
Actuation	Hydraulic
Internal ratios and mph/1000 rpm	
Top	0.863:1/18.3
4th	1.042:1/15.2
3rd	1.454:1/10.9
2nd	2.235:1/7.1
1st	3.583:1/4.4
Rev	3.714:1
Final drive	4.076:1

BODY/CHASSIS

Construction	Unitary all-steel
Protection	Zinc-based paint to joints before welding; phosphating; electrophoresis (total shell immersion); pvc layer to underbody and lower body panels

SUSPENSION

Front	Independent by MacPherson struts, coil springs, tie rods
Rear	Independent by MacPherson struts, coil springs, lower wishbone, track control arms

STEERING

Type	Rack and pinion
Assistance	No

BRAKES

Front	8.94 in discs
Rear	8.94 in discs
Park	On rear
Servo	No
Circuit	Split front/rear
Rear valve	No
Adjustment	Automatic

WHEELS/TYRES

Type	5J x 13 Alloy
Tyres	165/70 SR 13 Pirelli P3
Pressures	26/28 psi F/R

ELECTRICAL

Battery	12V, 45 Ah
Earth	Negative
Generator	45A alternator
Fuses	16
Headlights	
type	Tungsten filament
dip	80 W total
main	90 W total

Make: Fiat
Model: X1/9 1500
UK Concessionaire: Fiat (UK) Ltd, Great West Rd, Brentford, Middx TW8 9DJ. Tel: 01-568-8822
Price: £3910 basic plus £325.83 Car Tax plus £338.87 VAT equals £4574.70 total.

The Rivals

Two-seater and/or topless sports cars in this price range are rare: Datsun 260Z (£6,080), Lancia Beta Spyder (£5,720), Morgan 4/4 1600 (£4,347), Panther Lima (£6,067).

FIAT X1/9 £4,575

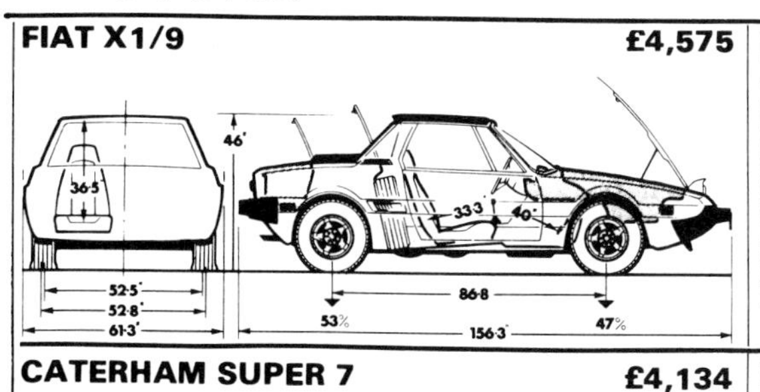

Power, bhp/rpm	85/6000
Torque, lb ft/rpm	86.8/3200
Tyres	165/70 SR 13
Weight, cwt	18.0
Max speed, mph	107.7
0-60 mph, sec	9.9
30-50 mph in 4th, sec	7.4
Overall mpg	29.0
Touring mpg	34.0
Fuel grade, stars	4
Boot capacity, cu ft	5.3
Test Date	Jan 27, 1979

The X1/9 now has the performance it deserves, from new 1500 version of very noisy, but revvy engine. Economy very good for the performance, aided by slick new five-speed gearbox. Handling and brakes still superb, with a good ride. New interior features better instruments, and glove locker, but new seats not as good as old. An excellent small sports car with detachable roof; great fun, and yet practical with it.

CATERHAM SUPER 7 £4,134

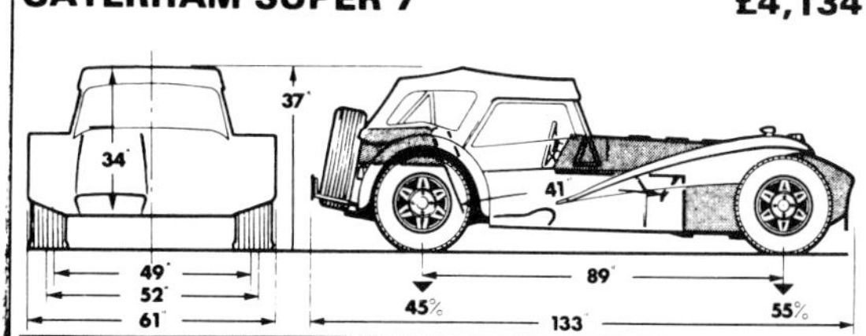

Power, bhp/rpm	126/6500
Torque, lb ft/rpm	113/5500
Tyres	185/70 SR 13
Weight, cwt	11.1
Max speed, mph	108.9
0-60 mph, sec	6.0
30-50 mph in 4th, sec	7.3
Overall mpg	†
Touring mpg	†
Fuel grade, stars	4
Boot capacity, cu ft	†
Test Date	April 1, 1978

†Not measured

Given a sunny day and the open road the Super 7 is a magnificent toy, with shattering acceleration, fabulous handling and superb close-ratio gearbox. Ride comfort quite acceptable for the type of car, but otherwise it's not an everyday car, with cramped interior, negligible luggage capacity, high noise levels, and poor visibility with the hood up.

MG MIDGET £2,971

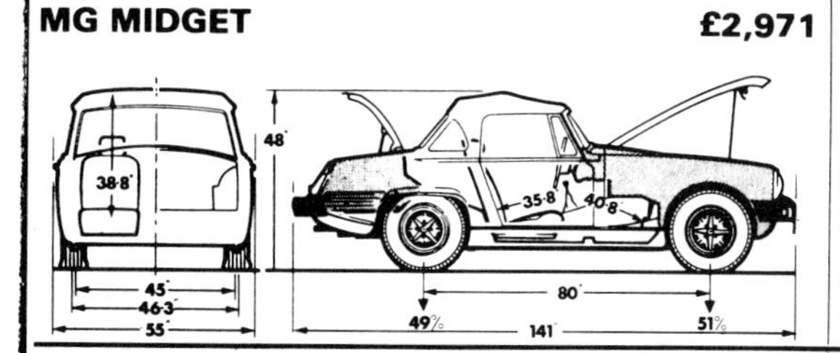

Power, bhp/rpm	65/5500
Torque, lb ft/rpm	76.5/3000
Tyres	145 SR 13
Weight, cwt	16.4
Max speed, mph	96.5
0-60 mph, sec	11.9
30-50 mph in 4th, sec	8.3
Overall mpg	27.3
Touring mpg	29.0
Fuel grade, stars	4
Boot capacity, cu ft	3.1†
Test Date	May 24, 1975

†Measured with boxes, not cases

One of BL's old-timers. Still a great fun car, but one changed by legislation rather than search for improvement. Now uses Triumph 1500 engine, which is torquey and economical. Handling still incredibly controllable but neither it nor (poor) roadholding improved by raised (US-spec) ride height. Cramped interior, and noisy, but beats the opposition hands down on price, providing cheap and economical wind-in-the-hair motoring.

MGB ROADSTER £3,996

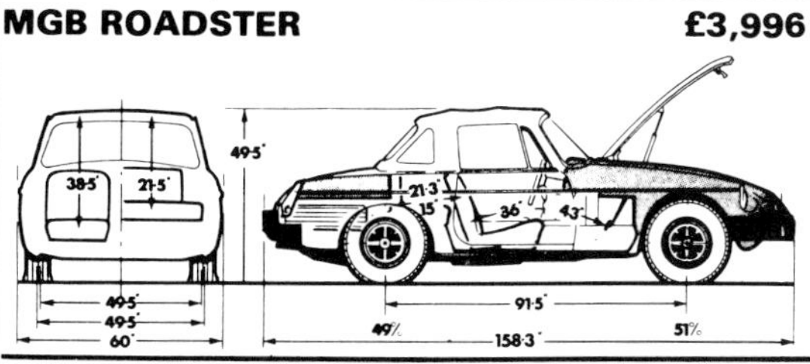

Power, bhp/rpm	97/5500
Torque, lb ft/rpm	104.8/2500
Tyres	165 SR 14
Weight, cwt	19.5
Max speed, mph	106.2
0-60 mph, sec	11.5
30-50 mph in 4th, sec	9.3
Overall mpg	23.5
Touring mpg	29.0
Fuel grade, stars	4
Boot capacity, cu ft	4.4†
Test Date	Jan 22, 1972

†Measured with cases, not boxes.

The other old man from BL's stable; laughed at by many for its ageing, heavy body but still selling well to those who appreciate reliability with soft-top motoring. Spacious and comfortable for two, and successive face-lifts have improved the interior and equipment and made the steering lighter. But many mundane saloons are faster and handle better. With overdrive, economy and high speed cruising are respectable, aided by well-fitting hood.

TRIUMPH SPITFIRE £3,365

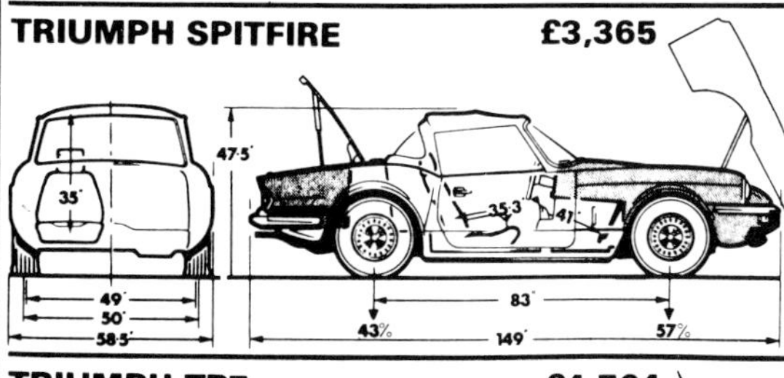

Power, bhp/rpm	71/5500
Torque, lb ft/rpm	82/3000
Tyres	155 SR 13
Weight, cwt	15.5
Max speed, mph	98.5
0-60 mph, sec	11.8
30-50 mph in 4th, sec	9.3
Overall mpg	29.8
Touring mpg	35.4
Fuel grade, stars	4
Boot capacity, cu ft	5.6†
Test Date	May 24, 1975

†Measured with boxes, not cases.

Yet another of BL's soft-top fleet using more powerful version of engine in Midget. Now handles quite respectably, with exceptionally tight turning circle. Long-legged gearing in overdrive makes for very good fuel consumption and relaxed cruising and d-i-y types will appreciate fantastic under-bonnet accessibility. Prettier, roomier and more civilised than the Midget and also relatively cheap.

TRIUMPH TR7 £4,764

Power, bhp/rpm	105/5500
Torque, lb ft/rpm	119/3500
Tyres	175/70 SR 13
Weight, cwt	19.3
Max speed, mph	111.2
0-60 mph, sec	9.6
30-50 mph in 4th, sec	7.5
Overall mpg	28.0
Touring mpg	31.4
Fuel grade, stars	4
Boot capacity, cu ft	7.7
Test Date	Sep 11, 1976

BL's controversial modern 'wedge' sports car is presently only made as a closed coupe, but convertible (and V8) versions must follow soon. Has earned a reputation for poor quality control but a good one is fun to drive with adequate (very torquey) performance and reasonable handling. Scores on comfort witn roomy, well heated and ventilated interior, nice seats, and comfortable ride, but let down by noisy engine and poor visibility. Quite economical.

OWNER'S VIEW

There seems to be no better way of learning owner's views of their X1/9s than talking to the enthusiastic individuals who lent their own cars for our photographic session – Brian Thompson, who owns a beautifully maintained ex-Fiat Auto (UK) 1300, and Joel Sciamma, who has owned his 5-speed 1500 from new. I let the owner of the earliest example talk first :

Brian Thompson, X1/9 enthusiast, and his 1300

AAGR: How did you come to buy your X1/9?
BT: I'd always been interested in sports cars – I got my first Lotus Elan when I was 20, then another Elan (a Sprint), then a Datsun 240Z. The Lotuses were very unreliable, so the 240Z was a reaction to this. After five reliable years with the Z, I wanted a change, and I wanted Elan-like handling, but better reliability. I read all the road tests, and decided that an X1/9 was probably right for me. At the beginning of 1978 the only decision was – new or secondhand. I actually bought mine from Fiat at Brentford, who were selling off ex-management cars. Mine is a 1977 model, and I bought it with 6,000 miles on the clock. Now it's done 45,000 miles.
AAGR: Has it been your day-to-day car ever since?
BT: Not always. Until 1981 it was, but then I bought a Fiat 126 to use for running about, and going to and from work. I'd picked up a couple of dents in the X1/9 due to street parking, and I was always worried about theft, too. I wanted to keep the X1/9 indefinitely by then, so now you could call it my hobby car, I suppose.
AAGR: What impressed you about the first X1/9 you ever drove?
BT: That was a demonstrator, not this car. I loved the roadholding but I was a bit disappointed by the performance (though it *was* a brand-new car), especially after owning a Datsun 240Z for so long.
AAGR: Was insurance a problem for you?
BT: No, not for me, I'd had sports cars for so long...but it can be a problem, I believe, for it's in the British Group 6, out of 9, especially for anyone under 25-30 years of age.
AAGR: You've had the car for more than five years. Has it been right for you in every way?
BT: The only slight disappointment is the odd bits of rust which appear after stone chips (quicker than I would have expected) – it's a constant battle to touch them up before rust takes hold....
AAGR: What about the handling, does it still match up?
BT: Oh yes. Having the Elan, I can still think back to the days when that set the standards. The X1/9's handling and roadholding is as good, you don't think about bends, you just drive flat out.
AAGR: What about traction, with the engine set back in the car?
BT: In the winter, I've noticed that traction is very good, but not remarkable.
AAGR: How is the car now serviced and maintained?
BT: I do it myself. But I can only check the tappets, not adjust them, because that needs sets of shims. My garage has only had to do them once in four years.
AAGR: Is the X1/9 a specialised car which dealers are afraid of?
BT: No. Basically, of course, it's a Fiat 128 with a Bertone body! Under the skin it's very simple, really. After all, Fiat only quote something like two to three hours for a major service. So it shouldn't actually cost any more to maintain than an average family saloon.
AAGR: So, you've had it for four years. What happens now?
BT: I intend to keep it...assuming it lasts. There's nothing out of the Ferrari class that I would really want to buy instead, not even a Lancia Monte Carlo; I've got a great respect for Porsche 911s, but that's out of the question....

Joel Sciamma, who owns an X1/9 1500

Joel Sciamma, bought his 1500 five-speed from new, and has come to most of the same conclusions :
AAGR: What was the reason you bought an X1/9?
JS: I was first very attracted to my car in the showroom, and it felt good and lively on the road. I bought it from new, and I've had it for more than three years. It's done 28,000 miles in that time – I restrain my use as much as possible!
AAGR: Had you ever had a sports car before?
JS: No, this was my first. In that style – mid-engined, modern shape – there's very little competition. Apart from the Monte Carlo, there's nothing, really.
AAGR: Has it surprised or disappointed you in any way?
JS: It disappointed me in one aspect – some of the detail design is odd; it's not uncommon with Fiats that you find rather unsuitable plastic ware, and badly thought-out wiring. But considering the price (about £5,000 new, four years ago), it is very good value. The bodywork in general is excellent, but details like seat coverings, for

instance, could have been far better. But everything functional is right – the handling, and the fun that can be gained are always a joy.
AAGR: What about mature reflection?
JS: Considering the cars I've had before, it has more precise steering than I would have thought possible, and it hasn't gone off at all with age.
AAGR: Do you find other cars trying to bait you? It looks like the sort of car which might infuriate others?
JS: Funnily enough, not other sports cars, but the XR3s, the 127 Sports and the Golf GTI's, they often try to prove themselves.
AAGR: Have you stepped back into what we might call 'conventional' cars, and terrified yourself? Is there that much difference?
JS: Yes, I drive a lot of cars – a lot of other Fiats too – and I always come back to the X1/9 to be pleasantly surprised by its abilities. But it hasn't got *the* highest standards of roadholding of any car I know – the tyres it has (165s) are far too small for that. My original tyres, by the way, were Pirelli P3s, which were atrocious in the wet – I'd have liked P6s, but I actually use Dunlops now, which are far more predictable. [Since I recorded this interview, Joel has fitted P6s, on special 5.5in rim Revolution wheels.]
AAGR: How easy is it to keep your car in trim? Is it easily maintained?
JS: Easy if you're familiar with it, but engine bay accessibility isn't good. Superficially it looks as if it should be sophisticated and difficult to work with, but many components are standard Fiat, and there's no problem in getting spares. There could be problems with the rear suspension, because dealers don't seem to understand that there is toe-in adjustment, and that must be *exactly* right.
AAGR: Has anything on your car worn out before you expected it to?
JS: No, nothing.
AAGR: Not a temperamental car then?
JS: No, but my experience with Fiats is that the engine needs to be worked hard. It doesn't like city work, and a lot of tickover – it seems to *like* being driven with a lot of verve. But it needs a lot of tender loving care – the major design philosophy is absolutely right, the detail is often lacking.
AAGR: Does the roof panel come off easily?
JS: Very easily indeed. It's not too heavy either – I often take it off by myself. I don't leave it at home, but usually stow it in the front, as intended. Really – it's worth taking the roof off, just for a 20-minute drive.
AAGR: What about insurance?
JS: It's only a problem for younger drivers, but the fact that it's Group 6 isn't too bad, because it's only a 1500cc; I'm in the IAM, so perhaps I'm a bit lucky.
AAGR: Tell me about the X1/9's anti-corrosion qualities. At three years of age, is your car showing any signs?
JS: The minute I got my car I had it rustproofed – an excellent job done with Protectol, by the way – and that has paid off. But the original rust-proofing looked inadequate to me. So perhaps I can't really tell you – but there isn't a spot of rust on it anywhere; but Brian is right, the nose is so low that stone chipping is a problem. You must then wax it immediately – personally I wouldn't touch up.
AAGR: How many of the black items on the car are plastic?
JS: Many of them – the engine air intakes, the bumper coverings, the base to the engine cover, but remember that the front spoiler on the UK-market 1300s is flexible rubber, not plastic. Everybody seems to get that wrong.
AAGR: Why do you think there is no X1/9 club yet?
JS: Probably because of the type of first owners of X1/9s, many of whom bought on looks, not because they were keen sporting motorists. There hasn't been a need for a club so far, but once the car is out of production, and true enthusiasts start buying them, that will be the time.

BUYING

Which Model

There really is very little to confuse the potential buyer of a Fiat X1/9. By the time this book is published, I suspect that the X1/9 will officially be out of production (see History), so the choice will very simply be between the original 1300 four-speed model (pre 1979), or the 1500 five-speed model built ever since.

There were, of course, several sub-derivatives, not all of which were marketed in every country. The UK launch models of 1977, for instance, had special trim, equipment, and goodies like fitted cases in the rear boot, while the pure black Lido model which followed was a French and UK model only. Even in 1982, there was the 'IN' model, mainly found in the USA, and the final 'VS' announced for the UK in the autumn of 1982.

Nor should there be any shortage of supply. Total X1/9 production was getting on for 150,000 examples, most of which should still be in existence – though the early ones, with their doubtful anti-corrosion record, may now be in a rather disreputable state. More than 80,000 X1/9s were sold in the USA, while by comparison British sales have been about 9,000 in all. A good many, of course, were sold in Italy, with most of the others scattered round Europe. British readers, therefore, will be disappointed to learn that only about six per cent of all X1/9 production was in right hand drive, though more than half of those were the later, 1500, model.

There is little choice to be made between the cars in terms of style, though the author prefers the looks of the original 1300, with its more delicate bumper and engine cover shaping, than the 1500 which followed. It is, however, worth noting that cars for the British market have usually been better equipped than those – say – for North America, and that quite a few British-market cars seem to have been loaded up with extras by their proud first owners.

Review of historical value patterns

At the time of writing, the X1/9 is still a model in current production, so that values of older cars follow the usual secondhand market pattern. Accordingly, the X1/9 has not taken on 'classic car' status, and there is no evidence of the old examples taking on the spurious so-called status of 'rarities'.

The 'limited editions' are really no more valuable than the normal production X1/9s, in spite of what the seller might like to tell you – a garage, certainly, would have no tendency to offer more for a Lido, or an early-launch car. With the price of a later model X1/9 (new) – in the UK – standing at nearly £6,500 in 1982, the availability of a five-year-old car for less than £2,000 is something of a bargain. Over in the United States, a 1974 X1/9 may be worth just a few hundred dollars, but it would need a great deal more than that to restore it to acceptable condition.

It would be foolish to offer a rigid opinion as to values, in a Superprofile which will be on the market for some time. However, because of the number of X1/9s in existence, which means that there will be no rarity for many years to come, the author would expect values for any particular model year to go on declining for years to come, which is bad news for current owners, but very good news for those wanting a value-for-money mid-engined sports coupe.

Problem Areas

The X1/9 is basically a splendid little car, but it has been built down to a price, and not to last indefinitely. As such a car gets older, therefore, it inevitably tends to corrode, and if this process has been neglected it may lead to a serious weakening of the strength and integrity of the structure.

Accordingly, any inspection of an X1/9 should begin with a close look at the structure. In particular, look underneath the car, when it is hoisted on a ramp, at the condition of suspension and engine pick-up points, and the sills, which add to beam strength.

Rust spots will now be in evidence on five-year-old cars, and more endemic on earlier cars (not sold, except in tiny numbers, in the UK), and evidence of corrosion usually breaks out first on the front wings, around the wheel arches, and along the door bottoms. Both the enthusiastic owners whose cars are pictured here warn of paint-chipping due to flying stones, so the nose of the car is obviously a critical area. There is, by the way, quite a limited choice of colours, *which are Bertone, rather than Fiat colours,* and some of the metallic paints have proved to be very difficult indeed to match after minor accident damage has been repaired.

Be sure that there are no obvious water leaks, particularly around the hardtop, which is removable. Even damaged rubber seals at this point can mean rain seeping around the edges.

Because most owners cannot see the front of their X1/9s from the driving seat, some cars have suffered bumper damage, and especially in the case of the 1500s (where the bumpers were more elaborate) it could be costly to have them replaced. The quality of seating materials, and carpets, incidentally, is none too high, so you should expect to find wear, distortion, or fading on cars over three or four years old.

Mechanically, the first thing to check is the chassis alignment – and you will soon know if this is wrong by taking the car for a test run; an X1/9 should be absolutely consistent in its straight-line running, and its left-hand or right-hand cornering behaviour. The pattern of wear on the tyres might also give you a few clues, as with any car.

Then it should be the turn of the engine/transmission assembly, for any serious work on the power plant will be costly as it is in a tight little engine bay, and not at all easy to work on. Has the car been properly maintained and serviced so far? And is there a service record to prove it? The engine behaviour, and the road performance, will soon show if the valve gear and carburation are in good trim, but poke around inside the bay to see if things like the hard-to-adjust fan belt is good and tight, and ask if and when the camshaft drive belt was last changed? (Fiat recommend every 36,000 miles).

Be very wary of any sloppiness in the gear linkage (there should be none), and if there is any tendency for synchromesh to have disappeared, this should only be on second gear.

Apart from alignment, there is little to go wrong in the suspension. The first signs of wear at the front will be bottom ball joints at the base of the struts, along with wheel bearings, while at the rear look carefully at the drive shafts. Shock absorbers should last at least until 35,000/40,000 miles, while front brake pads, depending on the way the car is driven, might last as little as 10,000 miles, which is no more than an average year's work for most X1/9 owners.

Beware, incidentally, of an X1/9 which has received very little use in the last couple of years ('collectors' cars' often spend much time sitting around waiting for their owner to get interested again, particularly if he has found something new to fascinate him...). One consequence of non-use is sticking disc brake calipers. You might also find that an X1/9 exhaust system, which is close to the 'splash' areas around the back wheels, may corrode quite badly – one would guess that most X1/9 silencers need replacing every two years or so, and that corrosion from the inside is often as bad as from road salt and filth.

Make sure that the specification and equipment of the car on offer is complete, especially down to the (removable) radio on the latest cars, and to the wheels and equipment on earlier 1300s. One of the joys of X1/9 ownership is the level of equipment offered – it would be a shame if 'yours' was deficient.

CLUBS, SPECIALISTS & BOOKS

Normally, in this section of a *Super Profile,* we also list specialists in a particular motor car, and the clubs set up to cater for it, but in the case of the Fiat X1/9 this has not only been impossible, but unnecessary.

At the time of writing, the X1/9 is still a current model in Fiat's lists (yet another special version having been shown at the British NEC Motor Show in October 1982), and it is a car which is well known to every Fiat dealer in Europe, North America and the rest of the world.

As far as the author knows, there is no specialist club catering for the X1/9. In Britain, at least, there have been two separate unsuccessful attempts in the last couple of years to set up such a club.

Books

Until relatively recently, there were virtually no books about Fiat cars, but this omission has been rectified in the 1980s. This is a representative list of books about the X1/9, and about the Fiat marque in general :

Forty Years of Design with Fiat, by Dr. Dante Giacosa.
Originally in Italian, but available in English, this is the story of Dr. Giacosa's distinguished design career at Fiat, which culminated in the early 1970s just as the X1/9 was born. A fascinating insight into the way Fiat management formulated its design policy, and the way that Dr. Dante Giacosa developed cars to their wishes. Published by Automobilia, published in Britain by Albion Scott.

Fiat X1/9 Owners Workshop Manual.
A complete practical guide to all aspects of X1/9 repair and maintenance.
Published by Haynes.

Fiat, a Pocket History, by F. Bernabo.
Small, literally pocket-book size, and no more than a thumbnail sketch of Fiat cars built from 1899 to the 1980s. Very little information on X1/9s. Published by Automobilia.

Books on the X1/9 are :

Fiat X1/9 : Autohistory, by Jeremy Walton.
A concise and well-illustrated story of the X1/9, stronger on flavour and impressions than on facts and figures. But Walton has driven and tested several X1/9s, obviously likes them. Published by Osprey.

Project X1/9, by P.B.S. Engineering of California.
This is not so much about the road cars, as about a Fiat USA-supported programme to turn the car into a racing machine. Well-illustrated, with exciting visuals, but too specialised for many X1/9 owners.

Fiat X1/9 Road Tests – 1972-1980, by Brooklands Books, compiled by R.M. Clarke.
The X1/9 covered in the familiar Brooklands Books style, 100 pages of pure reprints of British, American, and Australian road tests of the cars when new. No overall comment, and no attempt at a historial perspective. Published by Brooklands Books.

Road and Track on Fiat Sports Cars, 1968-1981.
Similar format to the above, also by Brooklands Books, but covering all Fiat sporting cars, and confining itself to *Road & Track* reprints. Published by Brooklands Books.

Also to be published in 1984 :

Fiat Sports Cars since 1945, by Graham Robson.
The author of this *Super Profile* has also written a comprehensive survey of all Fiat's famous sports cars, a saga in which the X1/9 plays a big part.
Published by Osprey.

PHOTO GALLERY

1. Bertone's Runabout Barchetta, shown at Turin in the autumn of 1969, actually had the elements of the X1/9's chassis underneath, but no-one suspected a thing. The production car was still three years away.

2. The interior of the open-top Bertone Runabout Barchetta was pure 'show car', and bore no resemblance to the X1/9 which was to follow in three years' time.

1

2

3

3. Fiat X1/9 body/chassis units being built by Bertone at their Grugliasco factory. Alfa Romeo Montreal body/chassis units, and the last of the 850 Spider structures, can be seen in the background, which dates the picture as early 1973.

4. The start of X1/9 body/chassis assembly by Bertone. Don't ever believe that modern coachbuilders make cars by hand – just look at all that welding gear!

4

5. This Fiat ghost view shows the remarkable packaging of the X1/9, with the 128-based engine/transmission packed into very little space behind the seats. The petrol tank is behind one seat, and the spare wheel behind another. The cooling radiator is up front, and there are sizeable luggage containers in the nose, and in the extreme tail.

6. One of the original Fiat publicity shots of the new X1/9, showing its smooth lines, the conventional pressed-steel wheels, and the big and rather obvious under-bumper air intake.

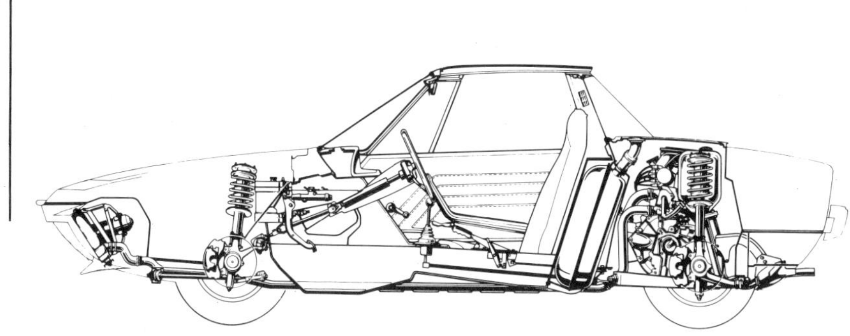

5

6

7

8

9

10

7. One reason the Italians liked their sports cars to have hard tops in the 1970s was that the weather in many parts was too hot to have the roof down! You can nearly see the heat shimmering off the seaside houses in this shot of an original (1972-type) X1/9 with pressed-steel wheels.

8 & 9. Top on and top off. This particular car, thought to date from 1974/5, belonged to the Haynes Publishing Group, who used it as the project vehicle for their X1/9 Owners Workshop Manual. *The car pre-dated official Fiat X1/9 imports annd had been converted to right-hand-drive in the UK. Note the changed pattern of the pressed steel wheels.*

10. If you can tear your eyes away from the lady for a moment, please note that the original UK-market X1/9s of 1977 had special decoration on the sides, and extra driving lamps. Note that the front spoiler was much larger, and separately coloured, compared with the very first cars.

11. *A 1979-specification X1/9 1500, complete with the rather large gear-lever handle, and the new facia and instruments. The roof panel has been removed to make this shot – a very easy, one-minute, operation.*

12. *An early publicity shot of the X1/9 1500, complete with 'five speed' badges on the tail, and road wheels sold to the USA but never to the UK.*

13. 1979-model USA-spec. X1/9 1500, with roof panel removed (note the fixing in the roll-over panel behind the seats), and those rather sexy wheels. From this angle the increased length, caused by the more bulky bumpers, is obvious.

13

14. Not too much room in the engine bay of the X1/9 1500, but enough to deal with all routine matters . The fuel filler cap can be seen at the top left of the engine bay, and the 'elephant's trunking' is to channel cold air to the air cleaner from the outside of the car.

14

15A

15A. 1981 North American specification X1/9. Note the new alloy wheels and the larger front side-marker lamps. This model featured electronic fuel injection and power windows were an option.

15B. Three Bertone-badged, two-tone X1/9s at the Geneva Motor Show in March 1982.

15B

16 & 17. The luxurious Bertone Fiat X1/9 VS.

16

17

18. *Cutaway view of the 1300cc X1/9 engine as used for the American market, complete with air pump to meet federal emission control limitations.*

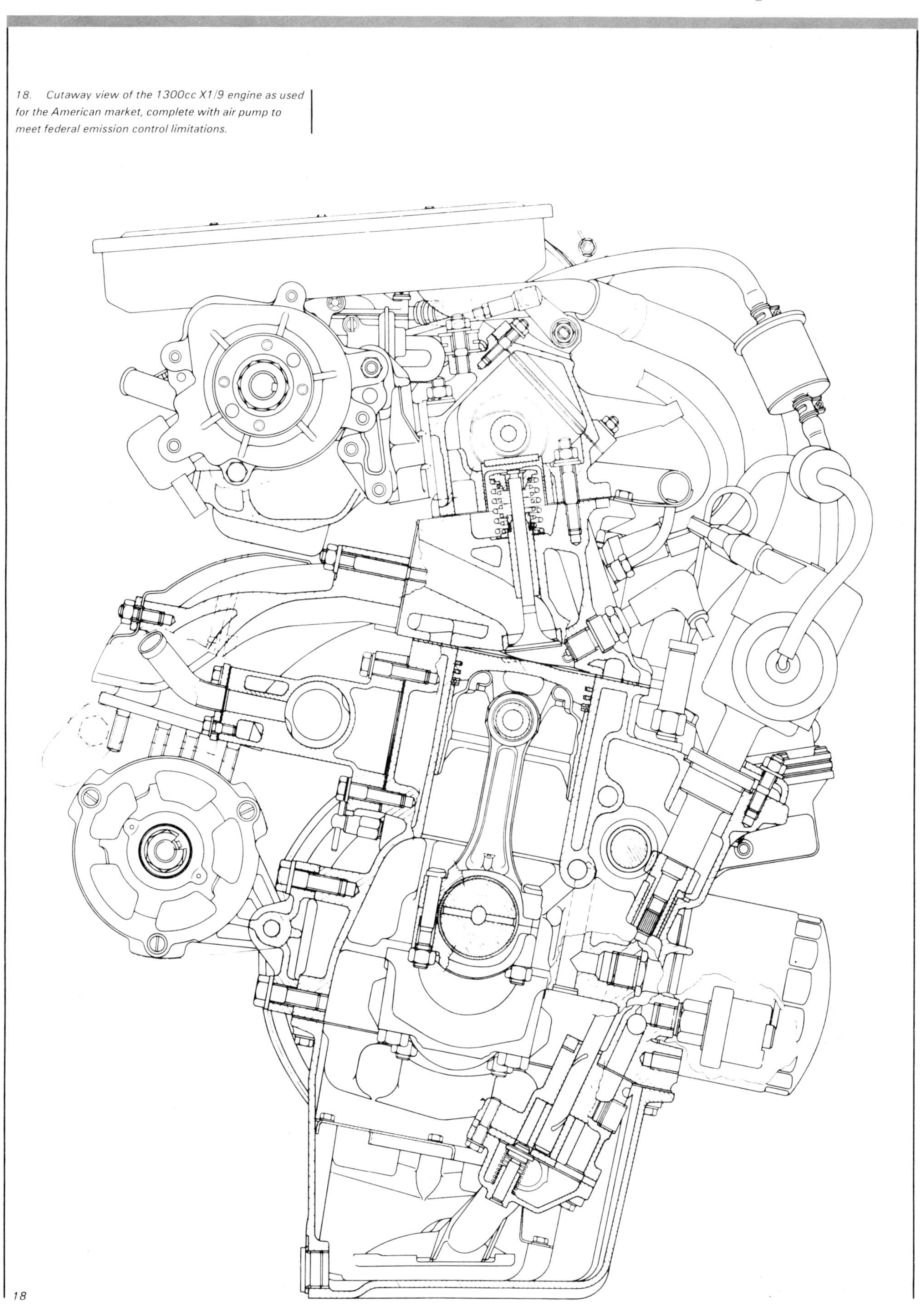

18

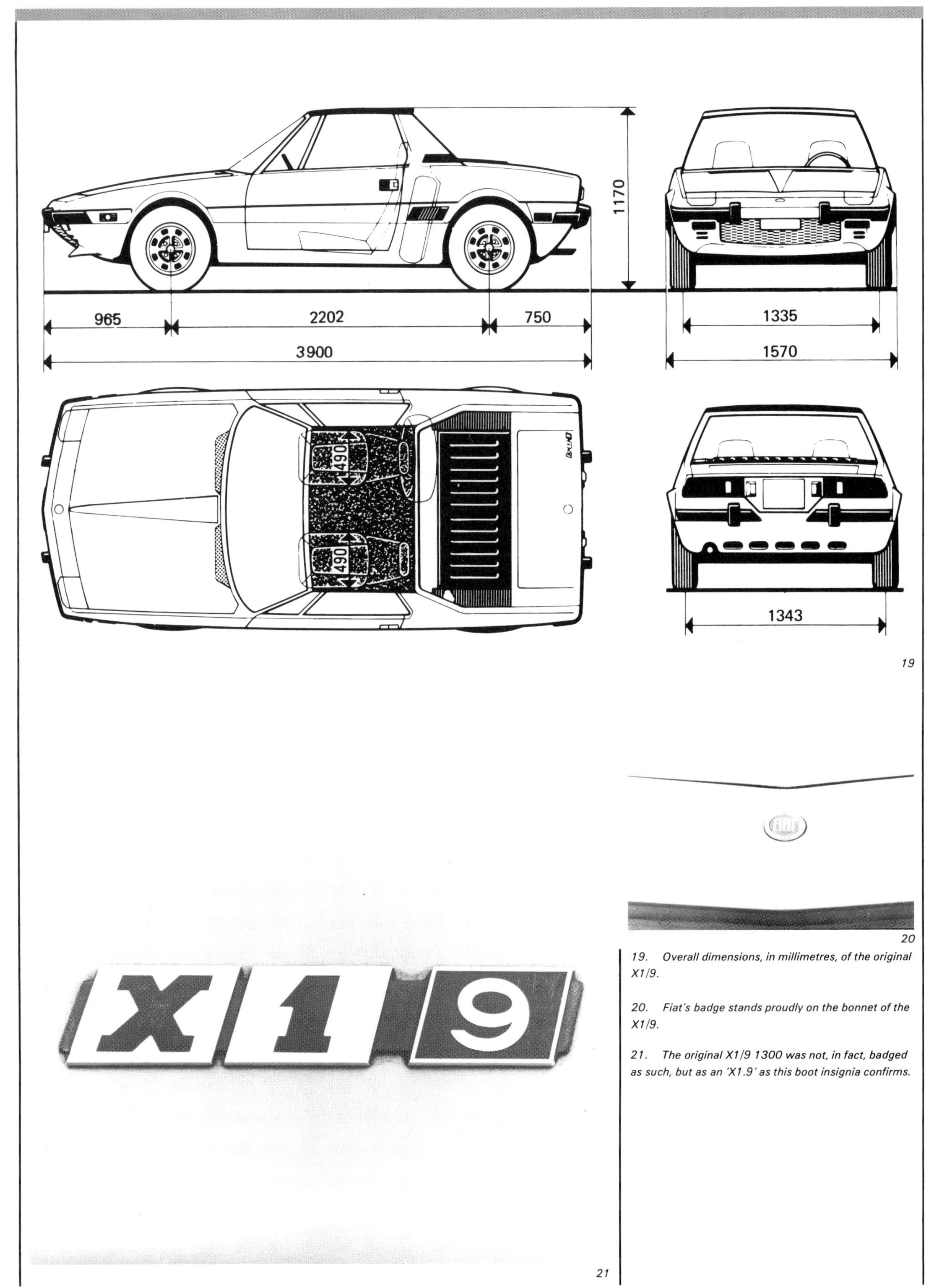

19. *Overall dimensions, in millimetres, of the original X1/9.*

20. *Fiat's badge stands proudly on the bonnet of the X1/9.*

21. *The original X1/9 1300 was not, in fact, badged as such, but as an 'X1.9' as this boot insignia confirms.*

22

23

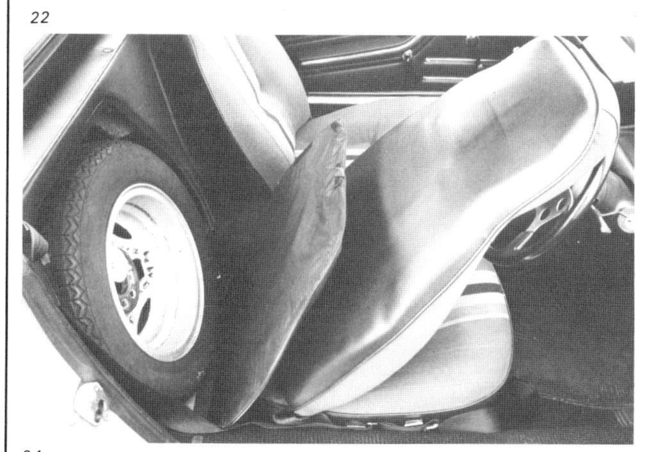

24

25

26

22. Fiat wanted passers-by to know that their X1/9 now had a five-speed gearbox.

23. Bertone's signature on the pillar of an X1/9, leaving no doubt of its parentage.

24. Ingenious stowage of the spare wheel on an X1/9. As designed by Bertone, of course, this would be behind the passenger seat on a left-hand-drive car.

25 & 26. Everything within hand's reach in the X1/9 'office'. This is a late-model 1300 showing the characteristic four-spoke steering wheel, the door 'furniture' and the striped seating of the period.

27

28

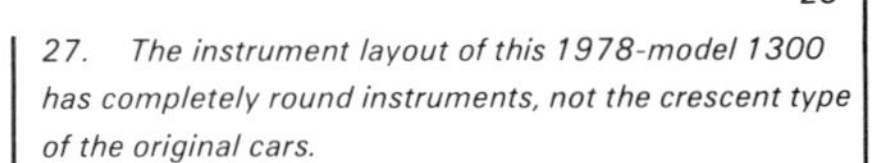

27. The instrument layout of this 1978-model 1300 has completely round instruments, not the crescent type of the original cars.

28. There was absolutely no space behind the seats of an X1/9 for stowage, for the fuel tank was behind the left of the bulkhead, and the spare wheel behind a panel aft of the right-hand seat. Note the very smart (and mildly impractical) white plastic seats on this gold 1500.

29 & 30. The facia and instrumentation of a 1500 were very different from that of a 1300, but on this 1500 a special accessory steering wheel has been added. The restyled facia of the 1500 5-speed included switches on a centre console. 1500s normally have a paddle-like gearlever, but this car has been mildly 'customised'.

29

30

31. The facia of the 1500 includes matching speedometer and rev-counter dials. On this car the rev-counter was set to rotate anti-clockwise as revs rose, but not all 1500s were the same.

32 & 33. Now you see it, now you don't! The roof panel of an X1/9 is detachable, and can be stored in the front boot of the car, in the catches already provided. In this case stowage space is a bit restricted, but not entirely obstructed.

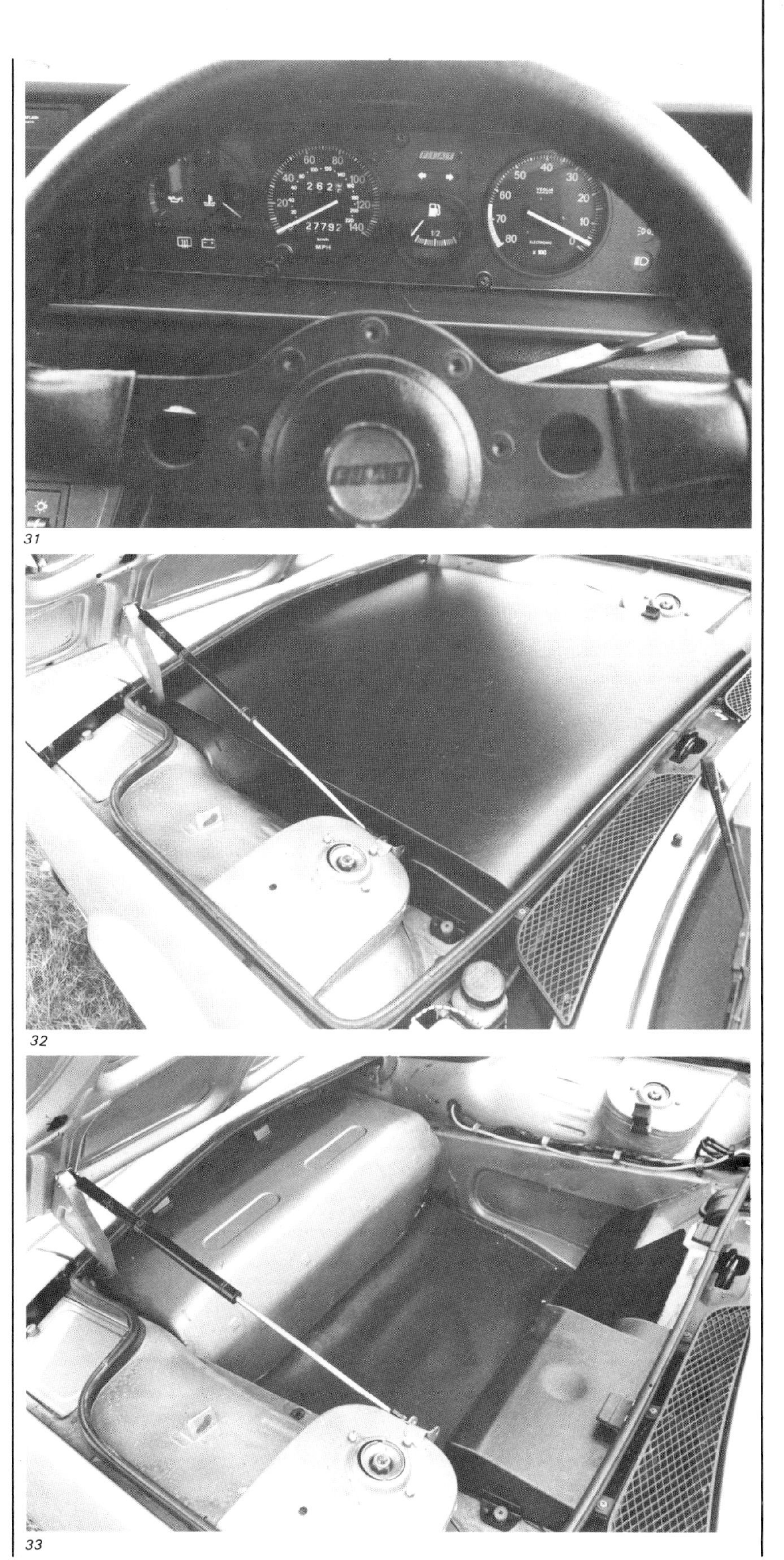

31

32

33

34

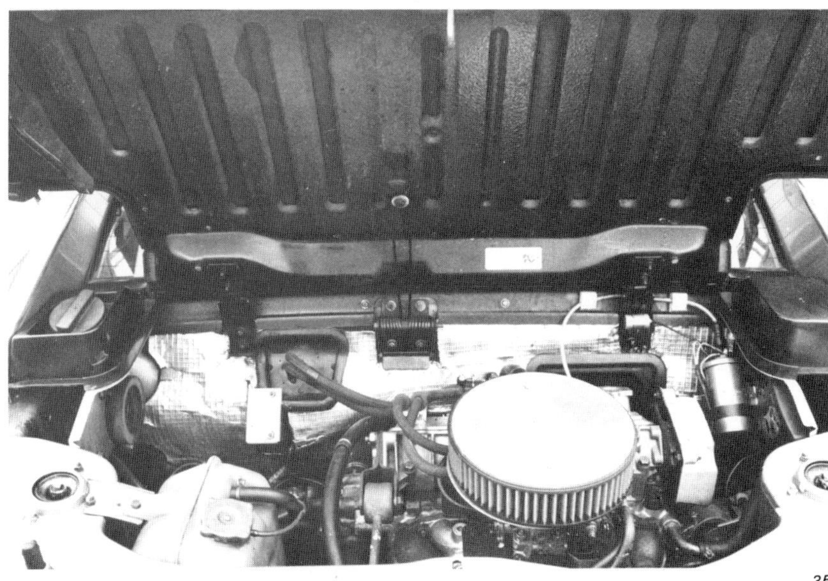

35

34 & 35. The engine compartment of an X1/9 is well-filled, whether 1300 (34) or 1500 (35). The Weber carburettor is hidden by that pancake air-cleaner, and the sparking plugs and distributor are tucked away next to the passenger compartment bulkhead. Note the difference in the size of the engine compartment lids and other detail differences.

36

37

36 & 37. To refuel an X1/9 you first have to find the filler cap. This is hidden away behind the nearside body 'flying buttress', next to the engine compartment lid. The tank itself is behind the left-hand seat.

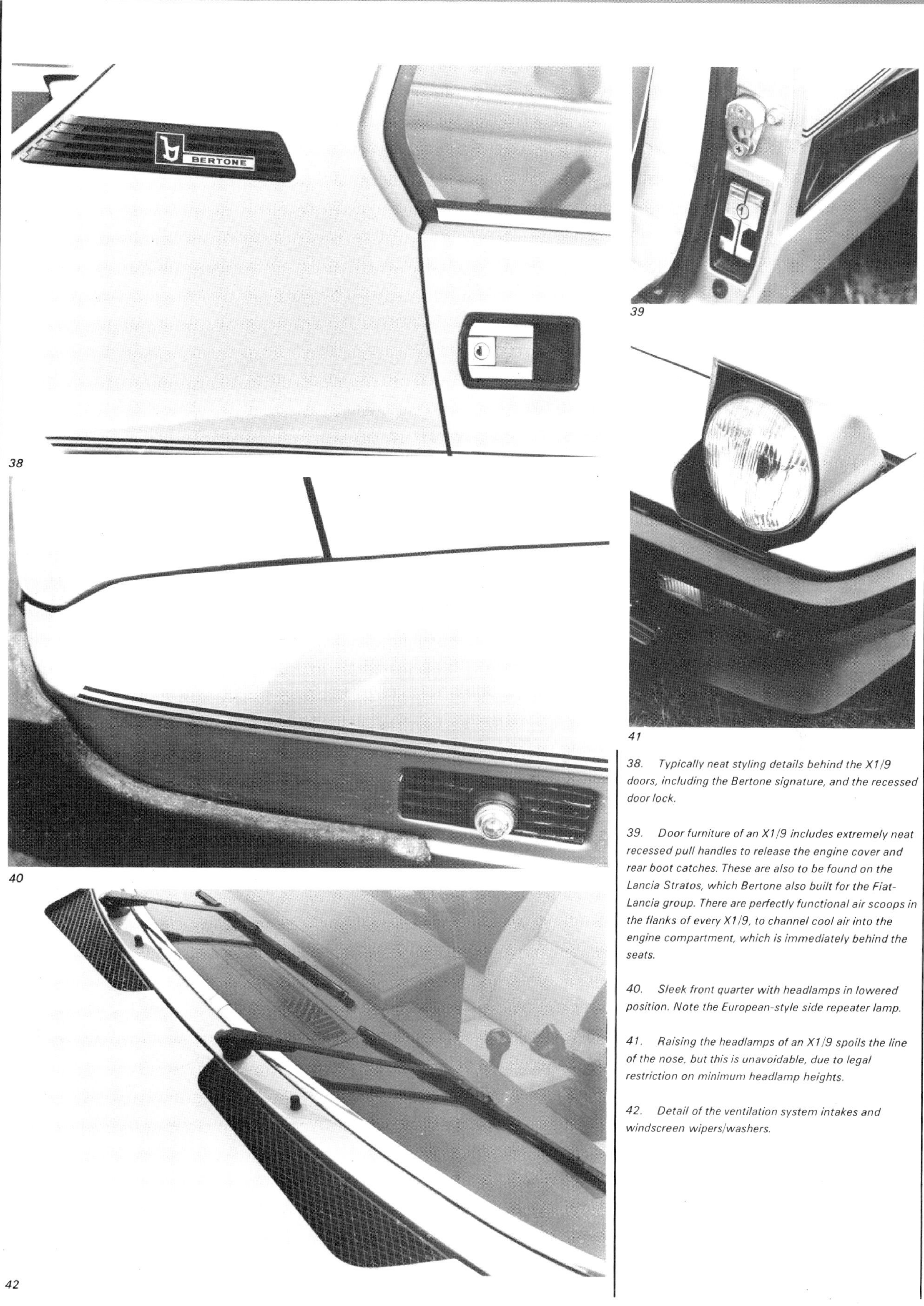

38 39 40 41 42

38. Typically neat styling details behind the X1/9 doors, including the Bertone signature, and the recessed door lock.

39. Door furniture of an X1/9 includes extremely neat recessed pull handles to release the engine cover and rear boot catches. These are also to be found on the Lancia Stratos, which Bertone also built for the Fiat-Lancia group. There are perfectly functional air scoops in the flanks of every X1/9, to channel cool air into the engine compartment, which is immediately behind the seats.

40. Sleek front quarter with headlamps in lowered position. Note the European-style side repeater lamp.

41. Raising the headlamps of an X1/9 spoils the line of the nose, but this is unavoidable, due to legal restriction on minimum headlamp heights.

42. Detail of the ventilation system intakes and windscreen wipers/washers.

43. Bertone's stylists even went to a great deal of trouble to make their number plate lamps neat and functional.

44. The distinctive light-alloy wheels of the X1/9 were standard on some markets (the UK for instance), but optional on others. The nuts are behind the centre cover.

45. The original X1/9 1300 not only signed itself 'X1.9' on the tail, but had a simple, not entirely full-width, engine compartment lid.

46

46 & 47. Difficult to make it absolutely right when US safety regulations intrude, but Bertone tries his hardest with the big-bumpered 1500. How many other cars would get away with bumpers and spoilers as big as this, and still look good? Compare the styling with that of the 1300 (47).

47

48

48. Some say the X1/9 1500 was spoilt by the bulkier engine compartment lid, but the bigger bumpers were certainly a styling success.

49 & 50. The 1500 5-speed is sitting slightly lower than the 1300, but this may be no more than production tolerances of spring lengths. Note the much more obtrusive door mirrors on the 1500 – and it has two, whereas the 1300 has only one.

49

50

C1

C1 & 2. *Sleek lines, uncluttered by any afterthoughts – this is a 1300, to British specification.*

C2

C3

C4

C3 & 4. Comparison of British specification X1/9s – 1300 (3) & 1500 (4). Note the larger and redesigned bumpers of the 1500 as well as its wider engine cover.

C5. The secret of Bertone's wonderful styling job was in its detail. A road's-eye view of the nose of the 1500 shows everything nicely in place – even those extra driving lamps, by Carello, look right.

C6. When the 1300 became the 1500 five-speed, the front bumpers were redesigned, and standardised for all markets. The 1500, with large bumpers, is the gold car, the earlier 1300 the blue car. Not only were the bumpers larger, but they increased the overall length of the car.

C5

C6

C7

C7. Full side view of the X1/9 1500. From this angle the wedge shape of this classic Bertone design can be fully appreciated.

C8, 9 & 10. Three different interiors. The 1300 (9) with its 'deckchair' striping and two special editions – the "IN" in dashing red and the "VS" in luxurious black. (8 & 10 courtesy of Fiat).

C8

C9

C10

C11

C12

C11 & 12. These two special editions of the X1/9 the "IN" (11) and the "VS" (12) look very similar at first glance. However they have different alloy wheels and, interestingly, the "IN" carries "FIAT" badges on the rear pillars.

C13

C14

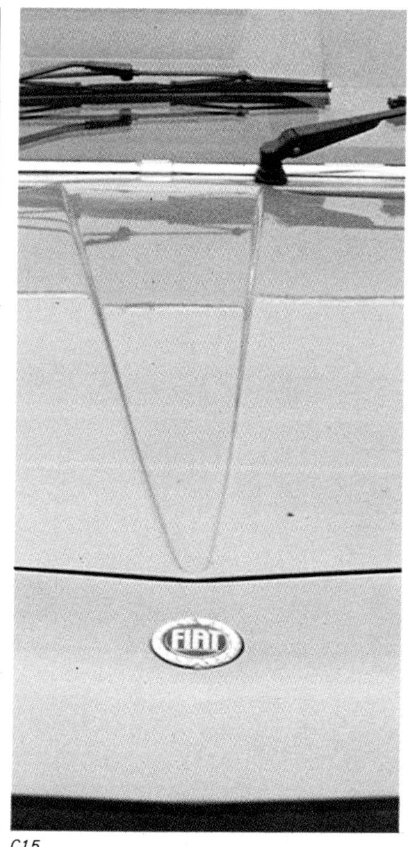

C15

C16

C17

C13, 14, 15, 16 & 17. Cameos of the Fiat X1/9 showing detail design in close-up.

C18

C18. This sunset provides an atmospheric setting for two X1/9s and emphasises the sleek and elegant lines which Bertone created for the world's most popular mid-engined sports car.